Cambridge Elements

Elements in Language, Gender and Sexuality
edited by
Helen Sauntson
York St John University

GENDER AND UPTALK IN HONG KONG ENGLISH

Wilkinson Daniel Wong Gonzales
The Chinese University of Hong Kong

Chan Pui Yu Ivy
University of Oxford

Zhang Xiaohan Harry
The Chinese University of Hong Kong

Ng Chui Yin Judy
The University of Hong Kong

Chung Yan Ching Karina
The Chinese University of Hong Kong

Shaftesbury Road, Cambridge CB2 8EA, United Kingdom

One Liberty Plaza, 20th Floor, New York, NY 10006, USA

477 Williamstown Road, Port Melbourne, VIC 3207, Australia

314–321, 3rd Floor, Plot 3, Splendor Forum, Jasola District Centre, New Delhi – 110025, India

Cambridge University Press is part of Cambridge University Press & Assessment, a department of the University of Cambridge.

We share the University's mission to contribute to society through the pursuit of education, learning and research at the highest international levels of excellence.

www.cambridge.org
Information on this title: www.cambridge.org/9781009634045
DOI: 10.1017/9781009634083

© Wilkinson Daniel Wong Gonzales, Chan Pui Yu Ivy, Zhang Xiaohan Harry, Ng Chui Yin Judy, and Chung Yan Ching Karina 2026

This publication is in copyright. Subject to statutory exception and to the provisions of relevant collective licensing agreements, no reproduction of any part may take place without the written permission of Cambridge University Press & Assessment.

When citing this work, please include a reference to the DOI 10.1017/9781009634083

First published 2026

A catalogue record for this publication is available from the British Library

A Cataloging-in-Publication data record for this Element is available from the Library of Congress

ISBN 978-1-009-63404-5 Hardback
ISBN 978-1-009-63406-9 Paperback
ISSN 2634-8772 (online)
ISSN 2634-8764 (print)

Additional resources for this publication at www.cambridge.org/Gonzales

Cambridge University Press & Assessment has no responsibility for the persistence or accuracy of URLs for external or third-party internet websites referred to in this publication and does not guarantee that any content on such websites is, or will remain, accurate or appropriate.

For EU product safety concerns, contact us at Calle de José Abascal, 56, 1°, 28003 Madrid, Spain, or email eugpsr@cambridge.org

Gender and Uptalk in Hong Kong English

Elements in Language, Gender and Sexuality

DOI: 10.1017/9781009634083
First published online: February 2026

Wilkinson Daniel Wong Gonzales
The Chinese University of Hong Kong

Chan Pui Yu Ivy
University of Oxford

Zhang Xiaohan Harry
The Chinese University of Hong Kong

Ng Chui Yin Judy
The University of Hong Kong

Chung Yan Ching Karina
The Chinese University of Hong Kong

Author for correspondence: Wilkinson Daniel Wong Gonzales, wdwonggonzales@cuhk.edu.hk

Abstract: This Element interrogates the complex role of gender in shaping the sociolinguistic variable of UPTALK within Hong Kong English, highlighting its interaction with other sociodemographic factors. Foregrounding gender as a central factor, the Element employs a robust array of methodologies to dissect how gender interacts with social factors, identities, and social types across a sample of sixteen participants. Findings unveil new perspectives on gender-dependent meanings of UPTALK, demonstrating that while gendered stylistic accommodation plays a notable role, UPTALK is not merely a gender marker. Instead, it embodies complex social meanings shaped by a broad spectrum of individual, cognitive (awareness), and contextual factors. By integrating both production and perception/attitudinal data from a relatively unexplored context, the Element provides a holistic, nuanced understanding of how UPTALK can function as a multifunctional sociolinguistic resource, offering insights into the theorization of language variation and social meaning, with particular focus on the role of gender.

Keywords: uptalk, sociolinguistic variation, experiment, Hong Kong English, construction of gender

© Wilkinson Daniel Wong Gonzales, Chan Pui Yu Ivy, Zhang Xiaohan Harry, Ng Chui Yin Judy, and Chung Yan Ching Karina 2026

ISBNs: 9781009634045 (HB), 9781009634069 (PB), 9781009634083 (OC)
ISSNs: 2634-8772 (online), 2634-8764 (print)

Contents

1 Introduction ... 1

2 Background ... 4

3 Hypotheses ... 9

4 Methodology ... 10

5 Results and Discussion ... 28

6 Comparison of Quantitative and Qualitative Data ... 74

7 General Discussion ... 76

8 Conclusion ... 81

References ... 85

An online supplementary material is available at www.cambridge.org/Gonzales

Gender and Uptalk in Hong Kong English

1 Introduction

High rising terminals (HRT), commonly referred to as "uptalk," refer to intonational contours that involve a rising pitch at the end of a declarative utterance (Levon 2020). Essentially, uptalk occurs when declarative statements are produced with a rising intonation, phonetically resembling the pitch pattern of a question rather than the typical falling intonation of a statement. However, syntactically, these utterances remain declarative rather than interrogative. In English, its use is variable: Certain intonational phrases in declarative sentences may not exhibit it, as shown in example (1a), while others may incorporate a rising pitch, as in example (1b). In this instance, the term *virus* was identified using acoustic analysis software Praat with a pronounced HRT (Slobe 2018: 549). Under the sociolinguistic variationist framework (Labov 1972b), the use of uptalk (i.e., [+ uptalk]) and nonuse of uptalk (i.e., [− uptalk]) can be regarded as variants of a single variable. In this Element, we refer to this variable as UPTALK (2). In line with sociolinguistic literature, we use small caps (i.e., UPTALK) to refer to "uptalk" as a sociolinguistic variable that encompasses use and nonuse of uptalk, and regular text (e.g., uptalk) to refer to the phenomenon of rising intonation, as illustrated in (2).

(1)   a. *There is a pandemic that is rampant in this **country** ∅*
     b. *... and it's the sexy baby vocal **virus**↑*
       (excerpt from the show *Late Night with Conan O'Brien* where voiceover actress Lake Bell was featured to promote her comedy film in 2013; uptalk indicated with ↑ while lack of uptalk with ∅; analysis done with Praat) (Slobe 2018: 549)

(2)   UPTALK → [+ uptalk/HRT]
           → [− uptalk/HRT] or ∅

The UPTALK variable has often been a subject of interest in English sociolinguistic research due to its association with gendered meanings. One of the earliest and perhaps most well-known identifications of this connection between gender and language was made by Lakoff (1973), whose work remains a foundational reference in sociolinguistics. She identified linguistic features such as uptalk and the use of empty adjectives as part of what she termed "women's language," an ideological construct that reflects societal expectations about how women should speak. Lakoff's analysis, while based largely on introspection and folk-linguistic observation, was pioneering in its argument that women's linguistic patterns emerge as a response to systemic power asymmetries. She posited that features such as hedging, tag questions, and politeness strategies are strategies for navigating male-dominated interactions. Although Lakoff's work laid the groundwork for sociolinguistic research on gender, subsequent scholarship has moved beyond the dominance-based framework she outlined. Researchers have drawn on constructivist approaches, viewing gender as performative (Butler 1988) rather than as a fixed social category with predetermined linguistic correlates. This perspective frames gender as emergent through iterative linguistic and social practices, including prosodic features like uptalk (Tyler 2015), challenging static notions of "women's language" and emphasizing the role of discourse in the continuous reconstitution of gendered identities.

Researchers focusing on English within "Global North" (henceforth, Western)[1] contexts such as the United States, the United Kingdom, and New Zealand have discovered that the use of uptalk can serve as a stylistic resource to convey femininity; however, they also found that it can carry other various social meanings, including politeness, inauthenticity, excessiveness, lack of intelligence, and informality, depending on the sociolinguistic context (see Section 2) (Britain 1992; Kiesling 2005; Levon 2016, 2020). Beyond indexing individual social meanings, the use of uptalk has been identified as a significant marker of solidarity between speakers and is used as a stylistic tool in constructing a gendered persona, that is, the "mock white girl persona" (Slobe 2018: 541), a persona where "gender" intersects and cannot be understood without notions of race (i.e., "White-ness") and age (i.e., "young"), as well as class (i.e., "middle class").

The findings of these scholars generally coalesce around two key ideas: First, there is no exclusive, direct one-to-one correspondence between UPTALK (i.e., the use or nonuse of uptalk) and gender, and second, the set of social meanings in an "indexical field" (Eckert 2008: 453) – including gender-related ones – associated with uptalk varies based on cultural, community, and contextual factors. In essence, there appears to be no universally fixed set of (gendered) meanings attached to uptalk. Also, these meanings relate to and intertwine with each other in the varied performances of gender in society (e.g., the enactment of personae) (D'Onofrio 2020). It is also understood that, like other gendered sociolinguistic variables such as the use of falsetto (Podesva 2007), the use of (ING) (Gratton 2016) (e.g., *running* vs. *runnin'*), or fronted /s/ (Calder 2019: 31),

---

[1] In this Element, we acknowledge the contentious notion of "the West," commonly used to differentiate certain societies in Europe and North America based on presumed distinct economic, political, and cultural traits. This binary framework of "the West" versus "the rest" simplifies and perpetuates a colonial and Eurocentric legacy, suggesting a problematic sense of superiority. Although the term is laden with ideological ambiguities and reflects entrenched power dynamics, we decided to use "the West" (including derivations such as "Western" and "Westernization") in its geographical and sociocultural sense for ease of comprehension and familiarity within established academic and also folk discourse.

uptalk can interact with other social factors, such as profession, the perceived safety of the environment, or the projection of specific personae like "fierce queen," thereby acquiring different meanings and functions in diverse contexts (Podesva 2007; Calder 2019).

Despite our increasing understanding of the nuanced, intersectional, and context-dependent nature of UPTALK in recent years, its use and social implications remain relatively unexplored in "non-Western" contexts like Hong Kong. The gap prevents a comprehensive understanding of the variable UPTALK in *all* of its social contexts and hinders one from fully understanding how gender operates linguistically in Hong Kong. To date and to our knowledge, the only relevant work in this geographic region is that of Cheng and Warren (2005), which focused on general "rising tones" rather than exclusively on "uptalk" or rising pitch or rising terminals occurring at the end of intonation phrases. Their research indicated that rising tones were used to establish dominance and control and not gender, suggesting that UPTALK may not inherently be tied to gendered speech patterns, as is often assumed in Western frameworks. There was no clear evidence that rising tones indexed femininity or masculinity, as speakers of all genders exhibited similar tone choices. Given that dominance and control were identified as exclusive functions of rising tones in their study, it is plausible that UPTALK in Hong Kong may serve similar pragmatic functions, rather than being primarily linked to gender as often proposed in Western contexts.

However, a crucial question arises: What if we were to specifically and systematically examine rising tones at the end of intonational phrases, which, as mentioned in the sociolinguistic literature, have been associated with gender? If such rising tones do indeed carry gendered meanings, would we observe variations in their patterns and meanings within the unique cultural context of Hong Kong, where Chinese and Western influences intersect? Addressing these inquiries will offer one of the initial insights into the sociolinguistics of UPTALK in Hong Kong, shedding light on the potential range of localized and gendered indexical meanings associated with this linguistic practice.

In this Element, our primary objective is to investigate the role of gender on prosodic stylistic variation of UPTALK in "mainstream-style" Hong Kong English (henceforth, HKE), which we define here as the dominant form of English spoken in Hong Kong with influences from Cantonese. As will be detailed in the methodology section (Section 4), our initial approach draws from the first-wave Labovian variationist framework (Labov 1972a), analyzing "gender" through predefined but self-identified groups. Specifically, in this Element we focus on "female"-identifying cisgender individuals who were assigned "female" at birth (henceforth, female)[2] and "male"-identifying cisgender participants who were assigned "male" at birth (henceforth, male), acknowledging, of course, the contentious nature of this binary classification in academia and beyond, recognizing it simplifies gender to mere biological distinctions. Nonetheless, we employ this classification as an initial comparative framework, consistent with some established sociolinguistic research methodologies. We recognize the importance of extending our analysis in future studies to include a more diverse array of gender identities. We also employ a constructionist paradigm that puts individual experiences and identifications at the center. In the context of Hong Kong (and particularly our set of participants), this approach requires us to engage with the highly hegemonic binary gender construct. This methodology not only facilitates easier dialogue with classical sociolinguistic research but also enables our research to be attuned with local cultural dynamics and individual preferences on gender expression.

To guide our investigation, we pose the following questions:

1. Is UPTALK in HKE perceived to be gendered? If not, what is the range of social meanings attached to it, as observed in listener *evaluations*?
2. Does gender (i.e., speaker gender, listener gender, gender context/setting) condition the *production* of UPTALK in Hong Kong, as previous research suggests? If not, what other factors affect or moderate its use?
3. To what extent are patterns observed in UPTALK *evaluation* different from that of *production*? That is, could explicit/implicit awareness play a role?

2 Background

2.1 Social Constructionism and Accommodation

Our study primarily relies on social constructionism and accommodation theories to examine UPTALK, a linguistic variable that has been observed to be gendered in many communities across the globe. In recent sociolinguistic research, scholars have predominantly embraced a postmodern perspective on language and its relationship with gender. This perspective neither characterizes gender as something that entails essential(ized) gendered qualities (i.e., women should use women's language) nor presents it as a static outcome of early

---

[2] We should clarify that in this Element, we sometimes use terms typically associated with "sex" like "male" and "female" interchangeably with those typically associated with "gender" such as "men" and "women." This usage acknowledges the entanglement of sex and gender, particularly in Hong Kong, where distinctions between terms like "female" versus "women" and "male" versus "men" are not strongly emphasized. In line with variationist research traditions, there are instances where using "women"/"men" can be perceived as stylistically awkward (e.g., as adjectives), and similarly for "female" and "male" (e.g., using *the males*).

socialization (i.e., individuals socialized to be feminine will always grow up to be feminine) (Cameron 2003: 188). Instead, gender is something that is dynamically constructed and negotiated through social interactions with meaning-laden linguistic and semiotic resources. Language, along with other semiotic resources (e.g., hairstyle, clothing), can be agentively used to convey or shape one's gendered identit(ies) or enact gendered persona(s) in social interactions (Section 2.2), which coalesce to form the notion of "gender" we know today (Eckert 1989, 2008). An illustrative instance of a gendered linguistic resource is UPTALK, which has been observed to have indexical values related to tentativeness and uncertainty, which can then be further linked to femininity (Warren 2015).

In addition to social constructionist theories, this study draws on communication accommodation theory (CAT) (Giles 2016: 36) to examine stylistic variation. Communication accommodation theory posits that speakers modulate their speech in response to audiences by converging, diverging, or maintaining their linguistic patterns. This theoretical framework is particularly relevant given prior research demonstrating accommodation-like effects in studies of uptalk. Though not arguing for an accommodation approach, Levon's (2016) study in London provides critical insights into the variable and accommodation-like use of HRT by men and women in mixed-gender interactions. Men exhibit a higher frequency of HRT use in mixed-sex conversations compared to single-sex conversations, employing the feature as a discursive strategy to assert interactional presence and engagement. Rather than reflecting traditional accommodation to female interlocutors, men's use of HRT was found to serve to consolidate their participation and maintain interactional salience. In contrast, women deploy HRT primarily as a mechanism for managing conversational control and mitigating potential disagreement. Their use of HRT is thus less indicative of accommodative convergence and more reflective of strategies aimed at sustaining interactional harmony (Levon 2016: 157). These findings suggest that linguistic adaptation is shaped not merely by convergence toward the interlocutor's speech patterns but also by broader interactional and social considerations. The patterns observed in London may be indicative of similar processes in other mixed-gender sociolinguistic settings, such as those in Hong Kong.

2.2 Gender Identity and Gendered Personae in Hong Kong

Scholars have identified diverse gender identities and gendered personae in Hong Kong society, reflecting the presence of a wide range of ways in which gender manifests in Hong Kong. Before delving into how "gender" is realized in

Hong Kong, it is worth discussing "identity" and "persona" and the relationship between them.

Scholars have viewed identity as a distinct construct with psychological underpinnings (Kish Bar-On & Lamm 2023), frequently operationalized as being related to one's subjective understanding of self, group membership, and social positioning (Cruwys et al. 2016). It has been conceptualized as an "emergent product rather than the pre-existing source of linguistic and other semiotic practices and therefore as fundamentally a social and cultural phenomenon" (Bucholtz & Hall 2005: 587). Thus identity categories are not seen as fixed entities but rather as necessarily dynamic constructs that evolve through consistent practice and are shaped by changing sociohistorical and ideological contexts (Haas, Jones, & Fazio 2019).

Identity is often differentiated from "personae," which are the social roles or facades that individuals adopt and perform in different situations or specific group settings. Agha (2003) defines a persona as a social construct associated with distinct linguistic registers, styles, or manners of speaking. A persona embodies a way of being and acting that transcends mere social identity, manifesting as either an imagined or actual character (Johnstone 2017). In this context, personae are not direct reflections of individual identities or "selves" but rather serve as "characterological touchstones" (D'Onofrio 2020: 11) that individuals can adopt, modify, or discard as needed in various situations, such as the roles of "diva" or "fierce queen" (Podesva 2007; Calder 2019).

In contemporary sociolinguistic variationist research, identity is often described as ideologically interconnected with the concept of "persona." From this perspective, "identity" is considered a broader term that includes or is constituted by various social personae. These personae are interactional constructs that individuals use to conduct *recognizable* identity work within their social interactions; they are necessarily specified for macrosocial information like race, place of origin, age, class, sexual orientation, and of course gender (D'Onofrio 2020). The concept of "persona" broadens our understanding of social interactions beyond just macrosocial categories, local affiliations, or psychological constructs of (self-)identities.

Relating language and language variation to these notions, the idea is that any association of the use of linguistic variables with gender (e.g., UPTALK with femininity) is mediated by interactional personae like the "Valley Girl," and broader notions of femininity emerge from the ways in which these personae become "ideologically linkable with macro-social categories through interactional use" (D'Onofrio 2020: 7).

In the Hong Kong context, studies of language in relation to macrosocial gender "identity" are limited compared to Western studies. These studies tend not to put emphasis on (micro)language variables, focusing instead on (general) gender itself. These studies all agree that gender identities in Hong Kong result from an ongoing negotiation between societal "Chinese" and "local" gender norms and individual self-perception. For instance, Kam (2003) demonstrated in Hong Kong that self-identifying masculine women can reshape and redefine womanhood without necessarily abandoning it in favor of masculinity.

The discussion of gender identity in Hong Kong would certainly not be complete without discussing gendered personae in the region. Unlike local work on gender identity, work on gendered personae has placed more emphasis on the role of language. One of the most prominent local gendered personae is the *gong neoi* "Kong Girl" persona, derived from "Hong Kong Girl." While the Kong Girl persona originally referred to women in Hong Kong neutrally, it has acquired a negative connotation over time, becoming synonymous with being "materialistic, narcissistic, and demanding" (Chen & Kang 2015: 194). This persona has evolved into a stereotype recognized through both nonlinguistic traits like an obsession with food photos and linguistic features such as a higher pitch, code-switching between Cantonese and English, and excessive use of /r/ sounds (Chen & Kang 2015).

In summary, research on macrosocial gender "identities" and gendered personae in Hong Kong highlights the use of various semiotic resources in constructing them, revealing indexical links between language variables (e.g., code-switching and /r/) and social meanings such as entitlement and shallowness, which are then ideologically linked to femininity or "womanhood" via widely recognized and media-moderated personae such as "Kong Girl."

2.3 Gender and Language in the Hong Kong Context

Previous studies in Hong Kong have explored the relationship of gender with linguistic features, such as hedges, refusal strategies, and code-mixing. Wong (2006), for example, found that hedges were more frequently used by female speakers, attributing this to women's expected role in maintaining conversational solidarity. Wong (2018) studied how Hong Kong Chinese EFL learners made refusals in English, revealing that men and women employed different strategies. Men tend to use a combination of both direct and indirect strategies when making refusals. Women, on the other hand, mostly use indirect strategies only for refusing. Schnurr and Mak (2011) analyzed real-life workplace interactions and found that female leaders often used both feminine and masculine speech styles to navigate a male-dominated environment: They often display masculine leadership styles, such as directness and authority, while incorporating feminine elements like a soft tone of voice and inclusive language (e.g., "we" instead of "I") to mitigate the impact of their directives. Wong (2004) reported that female Cantonese–English bilingual speakers used more code-mixing, especially with female interlocutors.

However, these studies have faced limitations. Some, like Wong (2006) and Wong (2018), did not effectively disentangle the influence of gender from that of gender settings, potentially muddling the source of linguistic variations. Wong (2018) found that participants' native languages (e.g., Cantonese, Japanese) may have affected their language strategies, introducing potential confounding factors. Furthermore, participants' gender imbalances, as seen in Wong (2018), may result in skewed data, raising questions about the representativeness of the findings.

This Element aims to overcome these limitations by ensuring an equal representation of genders and a balanced number of participants, while also controlling for variables like language backgrounds and social status.

2.4 Uptalk in Hong Kong and Beyond

The variable UPTALK has garnered considerable interest in sociolinguistic research, with studies revealing diverse social connotations attributed to uptalk across various contexts.

In the context of Porirua, New Zealand, Britain (1992) found that the use of uptalk was favored by young Māori and young Pakeha women, suggesting that uptalk had acquired social meanings associated with youth, Māori ethnicity, Pakeha ethnicity, and femininity. Slobe (2018) investigates parody performances of the "mock white girl" persona in the United States. The research identified UPTALK as one of the semiotic resources used in stylizing the persona, along with features like creaky voice, blondeness, and going to Starbucks. The study found that exaggerated use of uptalk rendered the style excessive and inauthentic. Uptalk in this context was associated with whiteness, femininity, and the performance of inauthenticity and excessiveness. The findings highlighted the diverse interpretations and associations individuals make with the use of uptalk.

In the context of Hong Kong, UPTALK has not been directly explored. The closest work is that of Cheng and Warren (2005), who conducted corpus analyses on the use of rising and rise-fall tones in Hong Kong, focusing on HKE and Chinese. Their study found that intonation was influenced by discourse type and designated roles of speakers. Rising tone was found to be almost ten times more frequent among supervisors than supervisees. The use of rise-fall tones was infrequent but occurred more frequently in supervisor–supervisee interactions, particularly when discussing unclear topics. Rising tone (which we interpret as being inclusive of uptalk) in the HKE context was perceived as asserting dominance and control, with no salient gendered meanings observed. Speakers regardless of gender exhibited similar behavior in terms of their uptalk rates in the data investigated.

In addition to the social meanings and confounding factors identified in previous studies, the current study also speculates that one's "explicit awareness" of uptalk influences their use and interpretation of the variable. The notion of "explicit awareness" follows Labov's conception of "attention paid to speech" (Labov 1972a), which states that linguistic style shifts can occur when speakers' attention is drawn to them. For example, in his work, Labov directed the participants' attention to the pronunciation of "ten." The results showed that by making the participants more aware of the location of their tongue, participants were more aware of articulation and replied with more casual answers, showing that awareness could lead to style shifts. As such, the current study takes participants' awareness of uptalk into consideration when evaluating their usage and interpretation of the variable. This will be discussed in depth in Section 5.2.

Overall, the works reviewed demonstrate that the social meanings associated with UPTALK vary across different cultural and linguistic contexts. While some social meanings, such as youth and femininity, tend to appear somewhat consistent for specific regions, other indexical meanings of uptalk seem to be activated in various degrees depending on the community and cultural norms. They suggest that further research is needed to get a more nuanced understanding of UPTALK's social meaning(s) in specific regions and communities.

3 Hypotheses

This Element proposes the following hypotheses regarding UPTALK in HKE, motivated by prior sociolinguistic work and research questions, which are discussed in Section 2.

- H1. The use of uptalk will predominantly convey "feminine" connotations or meanings that could be ideologically linked and interpreted as "feminine." It will also have other meanings that are not necessarily related to gender (e.g., informality).
- H2. Gender will affect the production of uptalk. That is, women will use uptalk more frequently than their male counterparts. Gender will interact with other social or "extralinguistic" factors to condition UPTALK. The link between UPTALK and gender will be mediated/moderated by other macro-social factors (e.g., ethnicity).

H3. In conditions where speakers are explicitly aware of uptalk, at least some speakers of HKE will attribute "feminine" meanings to it. UPTALK will be mobilized differently in various gender contexts, for example, when conversing with individuals of the same gender compared to those of another gender.

4 Methodology

A mixed-methods approach was used to gain a more nuanced understanding of UPTALK in Hong Kong. Our methodology utilized a sequential design, commencing with the collection of quantitative evidence via a production experiment (Section 4.1) (Figure 1). Subsequently, we conducted an evaluation experiment (Section 4.1.4) followed by postexperiment interviews to gather qualitative data (Section 4.1.5). These qualitative data were later subjected to thematic coding and comparative content analysis (Section 4.2). The insights gleaned from this qualitative analysis (Sections 5.1 and 5.2) informed our statistical analysis of the quantitative data in Section 5.3, where we used both Bayesian regression analysis and random forests analysis complemented by a Boruta feature selection algorithm.

We will use both quantitative and qualitative data to examine all three hypotheses.

To ensure the integrity of our study, we strategically conducted quantitative data collection (i.e., production experiment) prior to qualitative data collection. This sequencing aimed to minimize speaker awareness and attention to speech, which have been found to influence speech patterns (Labov 1972a; Bell 1984). The rationale behind this approach is that in the last part of the qualitative data collection (i.e., postexperiment interview), we explicitly conveyed the study's objectives and asked participants to evaluate UPTALK, making participants aware of the variable of interest. Furthermore, in the first part of the qualitative data collection – the evaluation experiment – we asked participants to evaluate sentences that either have uptalk or not. Although we did not inform them that these sentences contain uptalk, the limited number of stimuli and lack of fillers could potentially prompt participants to be nevertheless aware of UPTALK, biasing the study as well. As such, we decided to conduct the (quantitative) production experiment before the two qualitative data collection sessions (i.e., evaluation experiment and interview). Had we conducted the interviews and evaluation experiment before the production experiments, participants might have adjusted their speech patterns based on this knowledge, introducing bias into the study.

The order of data analysis was also strategic: By conducting qualitative analysis before quantitative analysis, we aimed to gain insights into the factors

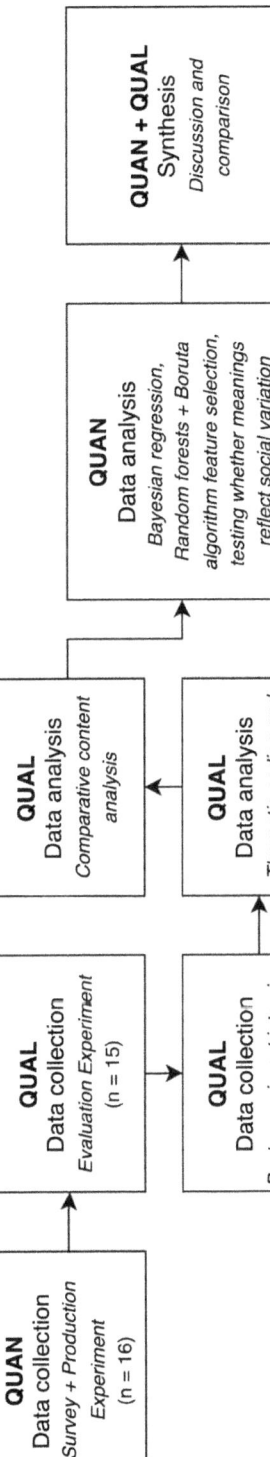

Figure 1 Procedural diagram of research activities in this sequential mixed-methods study.

to incorporate into our statistical modeling. Additionally, we sought to test whether the social meanings inferred from the evaluation experiment and interviews aligned with the social variation patterns observed in the production experiment data.

The entire protocol was vetted and approved by the Survey and Behavioral Research Ethics Committee (Institutional Review Board equivalent) of a public university in Hong Kong (SBRE-22-0753). This step was done to ensure that our study conforms to ethical standards in sociolinguistic research.

4.1 Data Collection

4.1.1 Participants

We recruited sixteen undergraduate students from Hong Kong to partake in our study, focusing on the impact of gender on UPTALK within this specific setting through an experimental lens. As such, our methodology was influenced primarily by the first-wave Labovian variationist approach (Labov 1972a), aiming to categorize "gender" into predefined groups. To determine participant groupings, we first conducted a preliminary survey with twenty-three individuals who had expressed interest in the study. Rather than using the common fixed-response format of "male, female, other" – which risks biasing participants toward binary categories and potentially marginalizing or "othering" nonbinary identities – we employed an open-ended question: *What gender do you identify as?* This approach allowed us to avoid assumptions about participants' gender identities and ensure that their self-reported categories guided our grouping decisions. All respondents identified as either "male" or "female." Based on these data, we randomly selected an equal number of participants from each of these two groups, centering our analysis on the predominant gender distinction that emerged within our participant pool: "male" versus "female." We acknowledge the contentious nature of this binary classification in academia and beyond, recognizing it simplifies gender to mere biological distinctions. Despite the complexity of gender and sex beyond simple binaries (Sauntson 2019), this goal of this study is to first establish foundational insights for subsequent research on gender and language in the HKE-speaking context. Our primary questions include whether binary gender influences uptalk and its association with perceived femininity or masculinity, aiding in future explorations of the dynamics between normative and nonnormative gender categories and UPTALK. We also want to emphasize that, in Hong Kong, the concept of gender is still highly heteronormative, intertwined with conservative Chinese ideologies and culture that enforce such a binary (Liong 2010). All sixteen participants, even with the option to identify outside the "male" or "female" categories, chose to identify within them. Adopting a grounded theoretical approach (Glaser & Strauss 2017), we respected the participants' self-identification. Overall, we found eight "female"-identifying cisgendered participants who were assigned "female" at birth (henceforth, female) and eight "male"-identifying cisgendered participants who were assigned "male" at birth (henceforth, male).

Although we do not anticipate that the university attended by the speakers would affect their usage of uptalk, we took precautions by balancing our data: Four males and four females were selected from one university (The Chinese University of Hong Kong), with the remaining participants chosen from another university (The University of Hong Kong). All the participants we recruited were aged between eighteen and twenty-five, a measure to account for potential impacts of generational shifts or educational backgrounds.

A combination of snowball and purposive sampling methods was employed for recruitment, drawing participants from our social networks. Some of these individuals were acquainted with one another, while others were strangers. Our deliberate decision to include participants with varying degrees of familiarity was motivated by our intention to investigate its potential influence on UPTALK as a factor in our data analysis.

4.1.2 Survey

After participants were briefed on the procedure and provided their consent, they were tasked with filling out a sociolinguistic survey. This survey aimed to gather various social information that we expected would condition the use of UPTALK, based primarily on our review of the sociolinguistic literature. The metadata we gathered in the survey include socioeconomic status (1 to 7, continuous), age (continuous), gender identity (i.e., "male," "female," "other," categorical), ethnic identity or ethnicity (degree of Chinese orientation, continuous), and self-reported English proficiency (1 to 7, continuous).

The goal was to gather as much social metadata as possible prior to conducting the experiments and interviews. From this extensive list, we would later select specific factors, like those enumerated previously, to include in our quantitative analysis. Our decision on which factors to include in the analysis was informed by insights gained from the qualitative analysis of the evaluation experiment and the postexperiment interviews. For example, if the interviews mentioned English proficiency, then the data related to English proficiency would be extracted from the survey data and linked to the production experiment data for confirmatory analysis. This selection process would help us determine whether our qualitative findings aligned with potential patterns of social variation observed in the production experiment. However, recognizing that some meanings of UPTALK may not be in the explicit awareness of speakers and thus not surface in the qualitative interviews and evaluation experiments, we also included social factors gathered from our survey that may implicitly influence UPTALK (e.g., age, class, stylistic formality) and interact with gender to condition UPTALK (Eckert 1989), based on previous English studies on sociolinguistic variation.

Overall, the collection of sociolinguistic metadata through a survey enabled us to explore the relationship between UPTALK, gender, and other factors, helping us get a more nuanced understanding of the UPTALK phenomenon. The sociolinguistic metadata from the survey will be used to supplement the qualitative analysis of UPTALK evaluation, but it will be linked to the production experiment data (Section 4.1.3) and primarily used to derive (sociolinguistic) factors for the quantitative analysis or modeling of likelihood of UPTALK production.

4.1.3 Production Experiment

This experiment aims to gather data that can help us understand the relationship between gender and UPTALK in language production and pinpoint the role(s) of other nongender social factors in the production of UPTALK, examining to what extent these nongender factors directly influence the use of uptalk and to what extent they mediate or moderate how gender conditions UPTALK. We operationalize "gender" in this experiment as "speaker gender" and "gender context," attempting to examine whether the speakers' gender and the gender context condition UPTALK. "Gender context" was integrated into the design of the experiment in order to test the last hypothesis – to find potential evidence of gender-driven stylistic speech accommodation or the (agentive) use of UPTALK in various gender settings (i.e., single-gender vs. mixed-gender settings).

Prior to the experiment proper, we randomly assigned sixteen participants into eight single-gender (comprising male-male or female-female pairs) and eight mixed-gender pairs, forming sixteen conversation dyads (consisting of male-female pairs) (see Table 1). Each of the sixteen participants underwent both gender setting conditions, to enable us to make causal inferences. The numbers of male-male ($n = 4$) and female-female dyads ($n = 4$) within the single-gender dyads were equal. Given our focus on the effects of familiarity on the use of uptalk, we sought to balance dyads in terms of acquaintance versus stranger status during participant pairing. However, given the priority placed on controlling for gender, the final dyads pairing exhibited some imbalance in familiarity distribution, resulting in five dyads composed of strangers and eleven dyads composed of acquaintances (Table 1). Despite this limitation,

Table 1 Conversation dyad arrangement

Conversation dyad session (in chronological order)	Participants		"Gender setting" condition	Familiarity
1	Levi	Johnson	Single-gender (M-M)	acquaintances
1	Theodora	Tamara	Single-gender (F-F)	strangers
2	Levi	Theodora	Mixed-gender	strangers
2	Johnson	Tamara	Mixed-gender	acquaintances
3	Mason	Maya	Mixed-gender	acquaintances
3	Samuel	Yasmin	Mixed-gender	strangers
4	Mason	Samuel	Single-gender (M-M)	strangers
4	Maya	Yasmin	Single-gender (F-F)	acquaintances
5	George	Gabriella	Mixed-gender	strangers
5	Tyson	Hayley	Mixed-gender	strangers
6	George	Tyson	Single-gender (M-M)	strangers
6	Gabriella	Hayley	Single-gender (F-F)	acquaintances
7	Emery	Tyler	Single-gender (M-M)	strangers
7	Cecilia	Gia	Single-gender (F-F)	strangers
8	Emery	Gia	Mixed-gender	strangers
8	Cecilia	Tyler	Mixed-gender	strangers

diagnostic analyses indicate that our model remains robust. Specifically, the effective sample size (ESS) of 3,944 suggests that our posterior samples provide sufficient independent draws for reliable inference, while an R-hat value of 1 confirms that our Markov chain Monte Carlo (MCMC) algorithm has successfully converged despite the imbalance. These diagnostics affirm the model's stability and the validity of our estimates. Thus, while the dataset is not ideally balanced by familiarity, it nonetheless provides a strong empirical foundation for investigating the relationship between social familiarity and the use of uptalk.

Each member of the sixteen dyads was instructed to engage in discussions on any topic they wanted in a quiet room, specifically, designated rooms within university libraries. Half of the participants began with the single-gender dyad conversations, where they conversed with someone of the same gender, and then proceeded to engage in mixed-gender dyad conversations with someone of another gender. The other half of the participants followed the reverse order, starting with mixed-gender dyads. This sequencing was implemented to control for potential blocking order effects.

Each participant completed both single-sex and mixed-sex dyad conversations within the same day. Each dyad conversation lasted for roughly thirty minutes and was audio-recorded using recorders with a sampling rate of 44,100 Hz, which allowed us to conduct acoustic analyses (Section 4.2). During the conversations, the facilitator(s) intentionally removed themselves from the room to mitigate the observer effect.

In summary, the dyads followed the organization detailed in Table 1.

4.1.4 Evaluation Experiment

This experiment attempted to probe the social evaluations and, consequently, meanings that English speakers in Hong Kong implicitly associate with UPTALK. Although we recognize that gender intersects with other social structures (e.g., class, age), for this experiment, we attempted to simplify the experiment design and simply focused on setting up the experiment to gauge or "isolate" the conditioning effect(s) of gender on (non)gendered attitudes or evaluations toward UPTALK. In the production experiment, gender was operationalized as "gender setting" and "speaker gender." However, in this evaluation experiment, gender was operationalized as "listener/evaluator gender" and "speaker gender."

To investigate whether there are gender-based differences in UPTALK interpretations, we addressed the question of (1) whether male listeners attribute different social meanings to uptalk compared to female listeners (i.e., "listener gender"), and (2) whether listeners attribute different social meanings to uptalk by male speakers compared to female speakers (i.e., "speaker gender"). In recognition of the complexity of "gender," we also explored the potential interactions between the gender of the listener/evaluator and the gender of the speaker. Specifically, we compared how male listeners rate male speakers versus female speakers. Similarly, we examined how female listeners rate male speakers in contrast to female speakers.

Following the production experiment, the same participants were invited to take part in a recorded session via Zoom. The same participants were invited to enable us to maintain consistency in the data and to allow for a direct comparison between the production and evaluation data of this study. During the evaluation experiment session, each participant was presented with all four recorded audio stimuli once. In cases where the audio was unclear, participants were allowed to request a replay. Following exposure to each stimulus, participants were instructed to provide detailed, descriptive accounts of the speaker. This was inspired by the matched-guise experimental procedure in sociolinguistic variation studies (Mallinson, Childs, & Van Herk 2017). Unlike the matched-guise paradigm, in which participants rate filler or distractor stimuli to obscure the primary research focus by presenting speech as originating from multiple speakers, this experiment employed a more streamlined design. Participants were asked to evaluate only the target stimuli from two speakers, a decision made to mitigate participant fatigue, which had been a significant issue in our pilot study conducted one month prior. Despite the absence of filler stimuli, postexperimental informal interviews revealed that participants were largely unaware that the study focused on uptalk. Instead, they believed they were assessing speaker attributes, and notably, they did not realize that the stimuli were produced by only two speakers. Evidence of this lack of awareness emerged in the participant's choice of wording. Rather than specifying "he/she is trying to say the same line four times" or "both of them are trying to say the same line," the participant instead employed the term "all," inaccurately suggesting the presence of more than two speakers when only two were involved.

(3) *I think **all of them** are trying to say the same line. They recall for this purpose of meaning. Okay, yeah. (Mason)*

This suggests that the experimental design effectively maintained the intended level of perceptual naturalness and minimized potential demand characteristics.

Specifically, participants were instructed to infer aspects of the speaker's personality, mood, ethnicity, social class, and other relevant characteristics based on the audio stimuli. This approach was chosen over directly asking participants their feelings upon hearing the stimuli, based on pilot test results indicating that participants struggled with direct evaluations but found it easier to assess the speaker. Unlike classical language attitude studies that rely on adjective-based Likert scales for speaker evaluation (Campbell-Kibler 2010), we adopted an open-ended approach, allowing participants to provide spontaneous commentary rather than selecting from predetermined descriptors. This method minimizes bias and captures a broader spectrum of social meanings, including those that may operate below the level of explicit awareness.

We can conclude that the evaluations were influenced by uptalk, not the content of the sentence, since all stimuli contained identical text:

> *I think there is no inherent meaning in **life**, because humans are not tools like cups or tables, we are not born to serve a specific **purpose**.*

Among these stimuli, two included uptalk at the ends of intonational phrases, occurring in the words *life* and *purpose* (stimuli 2 and 4), while the other two did not exhibit uptalk in these locations (stimuli 1 and 3). To ensure that the stimuli were representative of HKE, they were presented to two native speakers of HKE, who confirmed their acceptability as characteristic of the variety.

Table 2 Stimulus conditions for evaluation experiment

	[− uptalk]	[+ uptalk]
Male speaker	Stimulus 1	Stimulus 2
Female speaker	Stimulus 3	Stimulus 4

Table 3 Phonological properties of [+ uptalk stimuli] (ERB = equivalent rectangular bandwidth)

	Stimulus 2 ("life")	Stimulus 2 ("purpose")	Stimulus 4 ("life")	Stimulus 4 ("purpose")
Absolute pitch rise of uptalk (ERB)	2.42	2.14	3.59	2.78
Total pitch rise of IP (ERB)	2.81	2.16	3.68	3.26
Relative excursion (ERB)	**0.86**	**0.99**	**0.97**	**0.85**
Absolute rise dynamism of uptalk (ERB/s)	8.02	5.51	8.42	6.50
Absolute rise dynamism of IP (ERB/s)	1.34	0.81	1.10	0.84
Relative rise dynamism (ERB/s)	**6.00**	**6.83**	**7.66**	**7.73**
Onset of rise (syllable)	12	11	12	11
Length of IP (syllable)	12	12	12	12
Rise alignment	**1.00**	**0.92**	**1.00**	**0.92**

To account for potential speaker gender effects, two sets of stimuli were created for the [+ uptalk] and [−uptalk] conditions. Half of the stimuli were produced by a young female-identifying speaker of HKE (stimuli 3 and 4), while the other half were produced by a young male-identifying speaker of HKE (stimuli 1 and 2) (see Table 2). Both speakers were in their early twenties, identified as native speakers of a "mainstream" variety of HKE, and shared similar socioeconomic and linguistic backgrounds. They were proficient in Cantonese, Standard American English, and HKE.

The phonetic properties of the [+ uptalk] stimuli were analyzed according to Levon's (2020) protocol, and were shown to be kept consistent (Table 3). Relative excursion indicates the degree of pitch rise in relation to the entire intonational phrase (IP). It is measured by taking the difference between the F_0 at the highest point of the rise IP and the F_0 at the onset of the rise elbow, which is the point that shows a clear upward trajectory of the pitch contour. The absolute difference is then divided by the highest and lowest F_0 of the entire IP. In addition to relative excursion, rise dynamism and rise alignment were also measured. Rise dynamism is the degree of pitch rise in relation to time, while rise alignment is calculated by dividing the syllable in which the uptalk begins with the total number of syllables in the IP.

The speakers were instructed to produce each stimulus six times (i.e., three times with uptalk and three times without) while maintaining a "mainstream" HKE accent. When productions did not meet the experimental criteria, coaching was provided, and retakes were required until satisfactory stimuli were obtained. Once candidate stimuli were produced, a single exemplar was selected for each condition (uptalk and nonuptalk) per speaker, resulting in a total of four finalized stimuli. The selection process involved consultation with the two HKE speakers mentioned earlier, who were knowledgeable about the phonetic characteristics of the variety.

To enhance experimental control while maintaining a natural and realistic quality (ecological validity), the focus syllables (i.e., those with or without uptalk) were extracted and spliced onto the alternate version produced by the same speaker. This process was designed to minimize extraneous variation while preserving the natural quality of the speech samples. While we recognize the importance of factors such as the rate of pitch rise (F_0), onset of pitch rise, and other prosodic parameters in studies of uptalk such as "rise dynamism" (Levon 2020: 49), we opted not to manipulate these features explicitly. Initial efforts to control for these variables across gendered stimuli in a pilot study yielded stimuli that listeners characterized as "unnatural" and "robotic," thereby introducing potential confounds rather than enhancing experimental control. Consequently, we opted not to impose strict controls on these prosodic variables, particularly given that the two [+ uptalk] stimuli were controlled to already examine gender effects. For example, prior research (Levon 2020) has demonstrated that fundamental differences exist between women's and men's average F_0 levels, underscoring the challenge of achieving perfect control without inadvertently influencing listener evaluations. Our pilot study further corroborated this concern, indicating that attempts to equate F_0 levels across gendered stimuli may themselves introduce perceptual artifacts, ultimately undermining the validity of the experimental design.

Given that this is an exploratory study, our primary objective is to lay a foundation for understanding the role of familiarity in uptalk use while maximizing ecological validity. Accordingly, inspired by Levon (2020), we prioritized the preservation of naturally occurring speech patterns *by gender*

Table 4 Block order by participant, gender, and university (* = did not come)

University	Participant	Gender	Listening order of audio stimuli			
A	Samuel	M	1	2	3	4
	Mason	M	2	3	4	1
	Theodora	F	3	4	1	2
	Tamara	F	4	1	2	3
	Yasmin	F	1	4	3	2
	Maya	F	2	1	4	3
	Levi	M	3	2	1	4
	Johnson	M	4	3	2	1
B	Cecilia	F	1	2	3	4
	Gia	F	2	3	4	1
	George	M	3	4	1	2
	Tyson*	M	4	1	2	3
	Emery	M	1	4	3	2
	Tyler	M	2	1	4	3
	Hayley	F	3	2	1	4
	Gabriella	F	4	3	2	1

over the imposition of rigid prosodic controls *across gender*, ensuring that our analysis captures speech as it is authentically produced in interaction. While this choice introduces interpretive complexity (e.g., different interpretations of UPTALK), particularly as perceptual responses may be influenced by variation in F_0 across stimuli, it reflects a commitment to ecological validity. This trade-off is an inherent consideration when working with spontaneous speech data. We expect that future complementary research would investigate the role of controlled prosodic manipulations in shaping listener evaluations, an important yet distinct line of inquiry beyond the scope of this Element.

To control for the carryover effect and order effect in the evaluation process, a Latin square design was employed in the presentation of the four stimuli per individual (Table 4).

It is worth noting that one participant, Tyson, was unable to attend the evaluation experiment and postexperiment interview due to personal reasons. Nevertheless, we retained his production data as the study's dyadic design made its removal problematic; excluding his data would require eliminating all dyad interactions involving him, potentially affecting the overall interpretation. In contrast, the evaluation and postexperiment interview did not rely on dyadic interactions and were primarily concerned with identifying broader patterns. Therefore, while Tyson's evaluation and postexperiment interview data were excluded, his production data remained integral to our analysis.

4.1.5 Postexperiment Interview

While the evaluation experiment explored implicit social evaluations toward UPTALK, the postexperiment interview focuses on the deliberate or explicit associations English users in Hong Kong make with it (research question 3). Following a bottom-up approach, it identifies explicit evaluations interviewees made that may or may not be gendered. By analyzing the data from the bottom up, the interview addresses the question of whether participants link gendered meanings such as masculinity or femininity with UPTALK without steering them towards confirming preestablished gendered notions. This approach facilitates a less biased exploration of participants' personal interpretations of UPTALK by minimizing external influence on their responses. It provides a more authentic and nuanced understanding into their social evaluations of UPTALK. These insights can reveal the social meanings tied to the variable, potentially including those related to gender.

The focus of the Element is on examining how gender conditions social evaluations or meanings of UPTALK. Therefore, instead of just focusing on general evaluations of UPTALK or the (gendered) meanings of UPTALK in general, the interview protocol was designed to explore whether the meanings of UPTALK made when people are explicitly aware of UPTALK vary according to the *listeners*' self-identified gender. In short, the interviews aimed to provide us insight into how the gender of the listener potentially impacts their evaluations of UPTALK when they are explicitly aware of the variable, building on sociolinguistic research suggesting that the social meanings associated with linguistic features depend on the context and the listener's background (Eckert 2016).

Before examining the extent to which explicit awareness influences the social meanings attributed to uptalk, the interview first investigates whether listeners can explicitly identify and comment on the feature itself. This approach aligns with Labov's (1972a) distinction between linguistic indicators, markers, and stereotypes, helping determine whether uptalk operates below the level of explicit awareness (as an "indicator"), is subject to stylistic variation and social evaluation (as a "marker"), or has become a socially recognized and widely commented-upon "stereotype."

The protocol of the interview was as follows: Following each participant's completion of the evaluation experiment, they immediately proceeded to a one-on-one interview. At the outset of the interview, participants were explicitly informed that half of the recordings they had heard during the evaluation experiment contained instances of uptalk. They were then given a concise explanation of uptalk, supplemented with illustrative examples to ensure comprehension. This step was implemented to confirm that all participant-listeners had a clear awareness of uptalk as a prosodic feature. After this explanatory phase, participants responded to a structured set of four questions. The first question was designed to assess explicit awareness of uptalk usage. The remaining three questions examined broader sociolinguistic awareness, focusing on participants' recognition of sociolinguistic patterning and the social meanings explicitly attributed to uptalk:

1. *To what extent do you use uptalk in your everyday speech? When do you use it most often?*
2. *Why do you think other people might use uptalk? And when would they use it?*
3. *Which people would use uptalk more often? Why do you think so?*
4. *If a person uses uptalk often in their speech, how would you evaluate them?*

When participants provided responses that were too general, ambiguous, or incomplete – for instance, characterizing uptalk as "feminine" – additional probing questions were posed, such as "Why do you believe women utilize more uptalk?" The interviews maintained a semistructured format, permitting deviations from the predetermined four questions as long as discussions still revolved around UPTALK or gender-related topics.

Since one participant opted out of the postexperiment interview, data from only fifteen participants out of the original sixteen were collected.

4.2 Data Analysis

4.2.1 Qualitative Data

Data Related to Explicit Awareness of Uptalk

The responses from the first question of the postexperiment interview (Section 4.1.5) were coded categorically and analyzed quantitatively to probe "awareness" of a linguistic feature, which is not usually a straightforward task (D'Onofrio 2018). In this Element, we adopt an indirect method to measure awareness. We first evaluate uptalk production for each listener based on a production experiment (Section 4.1.3), establishing an index that reflects the relative frequency of uptalk usage (Section 5.3). After explicitly defining and clarifying the concept of uptalk to participants, we asked listeners to characterize and explain to what extent they use uptalk in everyday English conversations (question 1, Section 4.1.5), which we coded into a five-category variable: never, seldom, sometimes, often, always. This is the actual frequency index. Then we calculated an index representing the relative *perceived* frequency of uptalk usage. From these two indices, we derived a measure of awareness by comparing actual and perceived uptalk usage: Larger discrepancies were interpreted as lower awareness. For instance, a listener with a low awareness index may report minimal uptalk use (perceived use) but actually uses it extensively, or vice versa. Conversely, a listener with a high awareness index would have a perceived use of uptalk that closely aligns with their actual use. The "match" between perceived and actual uptalk usage is quantified by the difference between the two indices related to awareness.

Data Related to Social Meanings of UPTALK

Qualitative data related to social meanings of UPTALK – that is, the evaluation experiment data (implicit evaluation – evaluations below awareness) and responses to questions 2 to 4 in the postexperiment interview (explicit evaluation – evaluations above awareness) – were analyzed qualitatively. The audio evaluations from the implicit evaluation of UPTALK experiment were transcribed and then coded for UPTALK (i.e., presence or absence of uptalk), "speaker gender," and "listener gender." Responses to the interview that are related to explicitly evaluated social meaning (questions 2 to 4), on the other hand, were transcribed and categorized based on listener gender, as, unlike the evaluation experiment, we opted for a more general approach and did not ask participants to specifically comment on the use of uptalk by male and female speakers, only asking them to comment on general uptalk use that they were exposed to during the evaluation experiment.

The transcribed and organized or categorized responses for the evaluation experiment and the social meanings part of the postexperiment interview were summarized and preprocessed for qualitative analysis. Descriptors and keywords (e.g., adjectives, social types) related to the speaker(s) who use UPTALK in the evaluation task and descriptors or terms related to UPTALK in general were extracted. There were instances when listeners would comment on or evaluate a non-UPTALK variable such as code-switching. Descriptors that involved these were excluded from the analysis. Descriptors that occurred in both "uptalk" and "nonuptalk" conditions were also excluded from the analysis to highlight potential sociolinguistic patterns, for example, the salient differences in social meanings indexed by "uptalk" and "nonuptalk" variants. To enable a consistent comparison, we normalized the terminology by grouping related terms or synonyms under a unified descriptor (e.g., "reluctant," "hesitant" > "hesitant"). We acknowledge that certain descriptors may carry subtle differences in meaning that are significant and should be preserved. Therefore, when any of the authors identified two similar descriptors as distinct, we opted not to combine them into a single concept. However, when all authors agreed on the merger, the terms were consolidated.

Once the evaluations were preprocessed, summarized, and standardized, we conducted a qualitative comparison of keyword evaluations. For the responses related to the evaluation experiment, we analyzed the responses by UPTALK condition. Apart from analyzing the meanings of UPTALK generally, we also analyzed the meanings by listener-participant gender as well as speaker gender. For the summarized responses related to the postexperiment interview, we analyzed the meanings by speaker gender in addition to analyzing the meanings of UPTALK in general.

To visually represent distinctions between gender variables, we opted to generate word clouds for both our evaluation experiment and postexperiment interview data, with larger words indicating higher relative frequency compared to smaller words. We decided to use word clouds for both types of data as it can facilitate an easier qualitative comparison between un-/sub-implicit evaluations of UPTALK versus explicit ones.

We anticipated that the findings of the word-cloud analysis may erase some of the nuances in social evaluations of UPTALK. As such, for the postexperiment interview data, we also conducted a modified form of thematic analysis (McKinley & Rose 2020) on the raw transcribed data. We initially categorized the interview data by the gender of the participant. Then each comment within these categories was assigned specific codes based on the prevailing themes expressed, such as the level of awareness or the educated meanings associated with uptalk. Following this coding phase, we attempted to connect and interrelate related codes to construct overarching themes that shed light on the nature of UPTALK and its explicit connotations.

4.2.2 Quantitative Data: Production Experiment

Preprocessing, Coding, and Subsetting

The audio recordings from the interviews were subjected to a preprocessing and coding process prior to quantitative analysis. First, the recordings were imported into ELAN, where they were segmented into IPs and transcribed into text. These audio-linked transcriptions were subsequently transferred to Praat for further analytical procedures. In Praat, we auditorily identified and coded declarative clauses and instances of rising intonation by leveraging acoustic cues – that is, each IP that we segmented was first coded for type (e.g., declarative, interrogative). Then, we did further UPTALK coding only for declarative phrases since UPTALK is predominantly salient in these phrases, and such phrases are often the focal point of research into UPTALK, presumably due to the relative ease of identifying instances of uptalk in these sentences compared to interrogatives or exclamatory sentences.

For the coding process involving declarative sentences, we annotated each IP for the presence or absence of a final rising intonation. This process involved both instrumental and auditory assessment. First, we examined the fundamental frequency (F_0) contours using Praat, visually inspecting pitch tracks for evidence of rising intonation at clause boundaries. This step served as an initial indicator of potential uptalk, though we remained mindful of pitch-tracking errors that can occur in F_0 extraction.

Following this acoustic analysis, we conducted an auditory evaluation of the utterances to determine whether the perceptual impression aligned with the visualized F_0 contour. In cases where discrepancies arose between the two analyses, the research team engaged in collective discussion to resolve inconsistencies. Our methodological approach was informed by prior research on uptalk (Levon 2020) but was adapted to fit the specific research questions and sociolinguistic context of our study. Each utterance was then coded based on a consensus approach. If all four researchers agreed that an utterance exhibited uptalk, it was assigned a coding value of 1; if none perceived uptalk, it was assigned a value of 0. In instances of disagreement (e.g., a two–two split), we consulted a trained linguist based in Hong Kong, who provided an expert judgment to resolve the tie. This multitiered approach ensured methodological rigor and reliability in our uptalk annotations.

Since we were interested in understanding the potential impact of social and demographic factors on UPTALK, we coded each phrase for the factors identified in what follows. The selection of variables in this study was informed by themes emerging from the qualitative analyses as well as insights drawn from the extant literature. Specifically, factors such as socioeconomic status, gender identity, English proficiency, familiarity, and sentiment of utterance were incorporated based on their salience in both empirical data and prior research. Notably, the inclusion of "tertiary institution" as a variable was motivated by research on vowel variation, which has demonstrated that university affiliation can serve as a predictor of localized phonetic patterns (Prichard & Tamminga 2012). In the Hong Kong context, the University of Hong Kong (HKU) is widely perceived as more internationally and Western-oriented compared to other institutions. This sociolinguistic perception suggests the potential for systematic differences in UPTALK production among HKU students, thereby justifying the inclusion of "tertiary institution" as a relevant factor in our analysis.

As for the choice to include ethnic identity as a continuous variable and not a categorical one, we used a continuous measure of ethnic identity to capture its fluidity and complexity, rather than rigid categories. This approach is particularly appropriate in a context like Hong Kong, where ethnic identity is often perceived as dynamic rather than fixed (Hansen Edwards 2016) – that is, many individuals do not see themselves as entirely Chinese or entirely Hong Konger, while some might say they are fully both. Prior research conducted in similar multicultural settings also show that higher ethnic orientation (EO) scores correlate rather than cluster with distinct linguistic patterns, supporting a gradient rather than binary distinction (Hoffman & Walker 2010).

1. Socioeconomic status (self-reported scale of 1 "low SES" to 7 "high SES")
2. Gender identity of speaker (male, female)
3. Age
4. Gender context (mixed-sex, single-sex)
5. Proficiency (self-reported English proficiency of 1 "low" to 7 "high")
6. Time (normalized to percentage scale)
7. Tertiary institution (Chinese University of Hong Kong vs. University of Hong Kong)
8. Familiarity (strangers vs. acquaintances)
9. Gender of speaker by gender context
10. Individual (random intercept)
11. Conversation pair (random intercept)
12. Awareness
13. Nature of statement (i.e., hard facts, personal experience, explanations, opinions)

The variables were derived or coded from a sociolinguistic survey they completed, which asked them to provide demographic data. The "sentiment" variable was derived using a *sentimentR* package that takes in a string of texts and outputs a value that corresponds to the level of positivity or negativity detected (Rinker 2022).

Our final dataset contained 4,854 declarative IPs, with a randomly selected 90% ($n = 4,368$) forming the training set for building a statistical model predicting uptalk likelihood and ranking factors, while the remaining 10% ($n = 486$) served as the test set, excluded from model fitting and used solely for evaluation. The model (see the following section on the Bayesian regression model) achieved an overall accuracy of 64.4% (95% CI: 59.97–68.66%).

We opted for a 90%–10% split instead of the conventional 80%–20% split to maximize training data, improving robustness and generalizability. This allowed the model to generalize over more data, enhancing its ability to detect UPTALK patterns. The model performed well, correctly classifying 272 nonuptalk and 41 uptalk instances, yielding a high positive predictive value (91.58%) – indicating strong reliability when predicting nonuptalk. The balanced accuracy of 63.44% (over baseline 50%) further confirms its effectiveness across both classes despite class prevalence differences. These findings underscore the reliability of the model and the robustness of the statistical patterns it identified, supporting the validity of the results presented later.

Using the training dataset, we employed two statistical techniques. The first was Bayesian logistic regression, which allowed us to identify factors that condition UPTALK, the extent to which these factors condition it (i.e., nonstandardized coefficients), and the likelihood of such conditioning effects. The second technique we used was Boruta algorithm with random forest modeling, which allowed us to identify standardized coefficients or the relative importance of the factors in predicting UPTALK.

Bayesian Regression

We employed a Bayesian mixed-effects logistic regression model, incorporating all previously enumerated factors as single, noninteraction predictors. To assess moderation effects of sociolinguistic and extralinguistic factors on the relationship between gender and UPTALK, we included interaction terms between "speaker gender" and selected factors: socioeconomic status, age, gender context, ethnic identity, English proficiency, time, tertiary institution, familiarity, and sentiment. Random intercepts for individuals and conversation pairs were added to control for individual and pair-level variability, enhancing our ability to detect extralinguistic effects. Bayesian regression analysis was conducted using the MCMC algorithm in the *brms* package within R. Each model ran 30,000 iterations per chain across four Markov chains. To ensure convergence, we followed Vehtari et al. (2021: 683), maintaining $\hat{R}$ values below 1.01 and ESS values above 400.

To evaluate certainty in effect presence, we used the probability of direction (*pd*) measure, which reflects the proportion of posterior draws aligning with the sign of the median estimate. A *pd* value close to 1 indicates high certainty in the effect's direction, whereas values near 0.5 suggest ambiguity (Makowski et al. 2019). While median values in Bayesian regression models indicate effect size, coefficients are not directly comparable due to differing variable scales. Standard scaling methods, such as centering and *z*-scoring, are inapplicable to categorical variables and could obscure critical details. Instead, we supplemented our analysis with the Boruta algorithm to rank variable importance in explaining and predicting UPTALK usage.

Boruta Algorithm

The Boruta algorithm, a machine-learning method for feature selection (Kursa & Rudnicki 2010), ranked variables by their importance in predicting UPTALK. It generated a shadow dataset – randomly shuffled versions of original variables – to simulate noninformative features. A random forest model then compares real and shadow variables to assess their predictive value.

Feature significance was determined using a z-scored mean decrease accuracy method where a variable was considered important if its z-score surpassed its shadow counterparts. To ensure robustness, the algorithm ran 200 times, minimizing randomness. The output ranked variables based on predictive consistency, using metrics such as median, mean, and maximum z-scores. It also calculated *normHits* – the frequency with which a variable outperforms its shadow. Features were classified as *confirmed* (reliable predictors), *tentative* (potentially predictive), or *rejected* (insignificant).

This study focuses on the relative ranking of variables, particularly gender-related factors, by examining the mean importance index, *normHits*, and Boruta's classifications. These insights, combined with Bayesian regression findings, enhance our understanding of UPTALK's social meanings and extralinguistic influences.

5 Results and Discussion

5.1 Evaluation Experiment

In this section, we report our findings for the evaluation experiment. To reiterate, because we did not explicitly ask participants to rate the utterances with UPTALK, the findings of this experiment can inform us about the meanings of UPTALK below the level of awareness (i.e., meanings associated with UPTALK when the listener is not explicitly aware of the variable).

5.1.1 Evaluations of [+ Uptalk] below the Level of Awareness

In general evaluations of [+ uptalk], many observers have perceived its use as indicative of a lack of confidence. Other negatively perceived attributes associated with [+ uptalk] include "lower class," "unsure," "hesitant," "less educated," "fake," and "uncomfortable." Conversely, positive perceptions of [+ uptalk] include "natural," "positive," "educated," "more friendly," and "careful." Additionally, the use of uptalk is connected to social meanings that are neither strictly positive nor negative, such as femininity (e.g., "female"), queerness (e.g., "LGBTQ"), and local identity (i.e., "Hong Konger"). These observations support our current understanding of variation in modern variationist sociolinguistics, challenging the outdated notion of a direct, unchanging one-to-one relationship between linguistic variables like UPTALK and gender. Instead, our findings illustrate a more complex, one-to-many relationship where the gendered meanings of UPTALK intersect with meanings of ethnicity, sexuality, and geography. It should be noted that while there is indeed evidence of gendered meanings of UPTALK in this evaluation experiment, most participants were not able to identify the gendered meanings of UPTALK when they were not

Figure 2 Summary of implicit evaluations of [+ uptalk] overall (word cloud).

explicitly aware of the variable. This is evidenced in Figure 2, where the meanings of "unconfident" and "uncertain" are notably larger than "female" and "women," meaning that significantly fewer participants identified gendered meanings compared to meanings related to stance.

Furthermore, it is also worth noting that listeners predominantly and implicitly ascribed more positive interpretations to [+ uptalk] than anticipated. Examples of such interpretations include high sociability, evidenced by descriptors such as "friendly," "kind," "outgoing," "easygoing," and "less aggressive." Additionally, although [+ uptalk] was associated with the lack of confidence frequently, as indicated in the larger relative size of "unconfident" in Figure 2, it is also associated with "confidence" and an overall positive sentiment. A subset of respondents also suggested that uptalk may signal leadership capabilities (Figure 2).

Our study also highlights apparent contradictions, like the simultaneous association of uptalk with both "confident" and "unconfident," as well as "educated" and "less educated." Within the framework of sociolinguistic variationism, such contradictions are anticipated, reflecting the inherent underspecification of language and the contextual emergence of meanings (Hall-Lew, Cardoso, & Davies 2021). These conflicting interpretations suggest that varying contexts might lead to different understandings of UPTALK. Consequently, we delve into an analysis segmented by different gender contexts, starting with the gender of the listener, followed by the speaker's gender, and finally examining the dynamics between genders of speakers and listeners.

Analyzing how listeners implicitly interpret [+ uptalk] based on their gender reveals some trends (Figure 3). First, it is important to note that the meanings associated with uptalk are fairly consistent across both genders of listeners, often conveying a sense of uncertainty, hesitation, or lack of

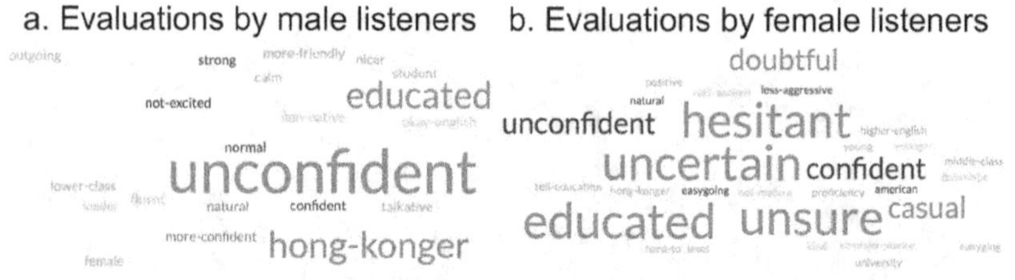

Figure 3 Implicit evaluations of [+ uptalk] by gender of listener (word cloud).

confidence (e.g., "unconfident," "uncertain," "hesitant," "unsure"). Second, the predominantly negative connotations linked to uptalk, as previously mentioned, were reported by female listeners. These listeners frequently equated uptalk with negative attributes like low confidence, using terms such as "uncertain," "hesitant," "doubtful," and "unsure" – with a significant majority holding this view, compared to a smaller fraction of male listeners who associated it with a lack of confidence. A second noteworthy trend is that female listeners often connect [+ uptalk] with traits typical of a higher social class, like being educated, middle class, and articulate, (Figure 3b) unlike their male counterparts, who primarily perceived [+ uptalk] as indicative of uncertainty and typical local "Hong Konger" speech rather than higher class attributes like being "educated." Some male respondents even explicitly labeled [+ uptalk] as lower class and "non-native." Last, it is important to note that while not as prominent, the interpretations related directly to gender, such as femininity, are solely emphasized by male listeners. This suggests a gender-based asymmetry in interpreting [+ uptalk], where male listeners implicitly subjectify the use of uptalk, and by extension, the speaker, to be feminine, regardless of the speaker's self-identified gender (Figure 3a).

When the data are analyzed according to the gender of the speaker rather than the listener, notable patterns emerge (Figure 4). First, the employment of [+ uptalk] by male-identifying speakers appears to activate implicit positive connotations associated with class, naturalness, and confidence. In contrast, these positive associations are diminished when [+ uptalk] is utilized by female-identifying speakers. Instead, the predominant interpretations involve a lack of confidence and certainty, accompanied by other negative evaluations such as perceptions of lack of intelligence (e.g., "dumb"). Moreover, interpretations that are not inherently negative, such as local-ness ("Hong Konger"), youth, and ambiguity (e.g., "hard to tell mood"), are also observed. These findings contribute to a partial explanation of the seemingly contradictory meanings previously noted with [+ uptalk], such as "confident" versus "unconfident." This variability in interpretation seems to be linked to gender presentations; uptalk, when employed in the performance of femininity, is often perceived by locals as

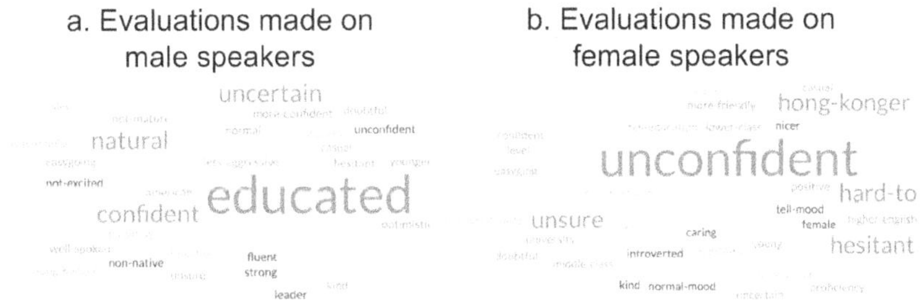

a. Evaluations made on male speakers

uncertain
natural
confident educated

b. Evaluations made on female speakers

hong-konger
unconfident
unsure hard-to
hesitant

Figure 4 Summary of implicit evaluations of [+ uptalk] by gender of speaker (word cloud).

a marker of lack of confidence, whereas its use in masculine performances is more likely to be interpreted as an indication of confidence.

Second, despite a general trend of attributing confidence to male speakers using [+ uptalk], it is important to acknowledge that some listeners still implicitly perceive signs of uncertainty (e.g., "uncertain," "doubtful," "unconfident," "hesitant") in the usage of [+ uptalk] by men. A more detailed examination of the data suggests that factors other than gendered identities might account for why [+ uptalk] is sometimes perceived as "uncertain" and "doubtful" even among male speakers. An analysis of other descriptors within the dataset provides additional insights. Alongside "confident," there are terms linked to leadership, as indicated by some participants labeling the speaker as a "leader" and using descriptors associated with leadership qualities such as "strong," "outgoing," "well-spoken," and "calm." The findings indicate that the confidence-related meanings ascribed to [+ uptalk] may be partially mediated by (gendered) social types. Among men, [+ uptalk] is interpreted as confident when the speaker performs a leader persona, but as lacking confidence when he does not. Intriguingly, the leader social type and related descriptors are almost entirely absent in the evaluations of [+ uptalk] used by women, suggesting the presence of potential essentialized gender stereotypes among listeners.

A third significant observation emerges upon closer examination: The primary meaning attributed to [+ uptalk] when utilized by men and listened to implicitly by listeners predominantly relates to class (i.e., "educated") rather than stance (i.e., "confident"). This differs markedly from its interpretation when employed by women, suggesting an interaction between the speaker's gender and social factors such as class and stance-taking.

Additionally, we found that the "ethnicization" of [+ uptalk] differs by gender at levels below listeners' explicit awareness. The use of uptalk has meanings related to "White-ness" (e.g., "American") when used by male speakers, but has meanings related to "Asian-ness" (e.g., "Hong Konger") when employed by female speakers. This phenomenon is evident in Figure 4, where "American" frequently appears in evaluations of male speakers, whereas "Hong Konger" is noted for female speakers, despite our efforts to control for accent variations. This finding implies that listeners may implicitly and ideologically associate masculine [+ uptalk] with notions of race/ethnicity, and implicitly, power. This potentially links perceptions of Whiteness with masculinity, education, upper class status, confidence, and leadership. In contrast, feminine [+ uptalk] is linked with Asian-ness, lower-class status, lack of confidence, and ambiguity, indicating the complex and multilayered interactive meanings of [+ uptalk] below the level of awareness.

It is thus challenging to assert that the use of [+ uptalk] universally signifies a lack of power, as previously posited by Lakoff (1973), especially in the context of HKE. The reality is that it is more nuanced. When [+ uptalk] is used by men, it appears to accrue more capital or power, as evidenced by implicit associations with Whiteness, upper-class status, confidence, and leadership – traits linked with power. Conversely, when used by women, [+ uptalk] seems to produce the opposite effect, potentially portraying the speaker as less powerful. Alternatively, this could be viewed as a different kind of power where [+ uptalk] by women is implicitly interpreted as enhancing sociability and pleasantness, as reflected in descriptors such as "friendly," "nice," "easygoing," and "positive."

Interaction effects abound in the implicit interpretation of [+ uptalk] when considering the gender of both the speaker and the listener simultaneously (Figure 5). Specifically, the analysis reveals distinct variations in the attributed indexical meanings of [+ uptalk] across same-gender and mixed-gender interactions. Male listeners tend to ascribe a "confident" and leadership-related persona to male speakers employing uptalk, whereas these connotations are notably

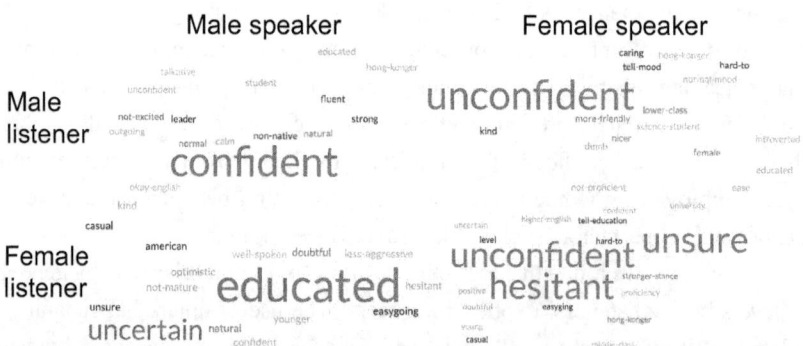

Figure 5 Summary of implicit evaluations of use of uptalk by gender of listener and gender of speaker (interaction) featured in the stimuli (word cloud).

absent when they assess female speakers using uptalk. Instead, [+ uptalk] by female speakers is predominantly characterized by male listeners as "unconfident," accompanied by less notable meanings such as "lower class," "more friendly," "nicer," and "dumb." In contrast, female listeners interpret uptalk in male speakers predominantly as "educated" with undertones of "uncertainty." When evaluating female speakers, however, female listeners attribute meanings related to lack of confidence, uncertainty, and hesitancy.

This pattern demonstrates a clear asymmetry: When not made aware of the uptalk variable, male listeners generally rate [+ uptalk] in male speakers more positively, whereas female listeners do not extend the same positive ratings to speakers of their own gender, often viewing their use of uptalk negatively. A similar disparity is evident in mixed-gender settings, where male listeners predominantly perceive female use of uptalk as negative, while female listeners tend to view male use of uptalk more positively. The findings reflect a stereotypical and naturalized positioning of women that is prevalent globally (Shen 2016), suggesting that through social practices such as uptalk, women are often positioned by men – and perhaps by themselves due to socialization – in a less powerful position.

Moreover, another key finding related to the complex interactions of listener and speaker gender in the context of [+ uptalk] relates to the variability in how male and female listeners implicitly evaluate female speakers' use of uptalk. Male listeners display less variability, frequently using descriptors like "unconfident." In contrast, female listeners use a broader range of descriptors such as "unsure," "unconfident," and "hesitant" to describe female speakers. Evaluations of male speakers also vary by the gender of the listener, with male listeners almost invariably describing the use of uptalk by men in Hong Kong as "confident," whereas female listeners are more likely to describe it as "educated" and somewhat "uncertain." These findings underscore the complex ways in which the use of uptalk is implicitly interpreted within different gendered contexts and stresses the importance of not essentializing gender through language in the context of Hong Kong.

5.2 Postexperiment Interview: Examining the Role of Explicit Awareness

The principal aim of the postexperiment interview was to examine the role of explicit awareness in the use and interpretation of uptalk. We define "awareness" as "explicit awareness," following Labov's notion of "attention paid to speech" (Labov 1972a; D'Onofrio 2018: 261). However, Labov's model of "attention-to-speech" is a continuum rather than a binary distinction, raising the question: Where does "explicit awareness" fall along this cline? To address this, we situate our discussion within Labov's framework of indicators, markers, and stereotypes, which captures varying levels of social awareness and salience in linguistic variation.

Our inquiry focuses on listeners' responses, commentary, and the social meanings they attribute to uptalk when explicitly made aware of it. This involves defining "uptalk," presenting examples, and soliciting evaluations based on utterances from the preceding experiment. Given Labov's framework, we assess whether uptalk functions as an indicator (below explicit awareness), a marker (socially evaluated but not explicitly noted), or a stereotype (highly salient and widely recognized). We analyze explicit awareness of uptalk along two dimensions: listeners' recognition of their own uptalk use and their explicit social evaluations of the feature. We first examine the extent of listeners' awareness and its placement on Labov's continuum. Then we explore the meanings assigned to uptalk when attention is drawn to it, considering whether this shifts its status as an indicator, marker, or stereotype.

5.2.1 Awareness of Uptalk

To what extent are the listener-participants aware of their use of uptalk? The data reveal varying levels of awareness among participants. Generally, most participants are explicitly aware of their uptalk usage – that is, they neither overestimate nor underestimate it (Section 5.3). Both visual inspection and descriptive statistical analysis (Figure 6, Table 5) indicate a slight rightward skewness in the data (skew = 0.23). Additionally, both the average and median values are positive

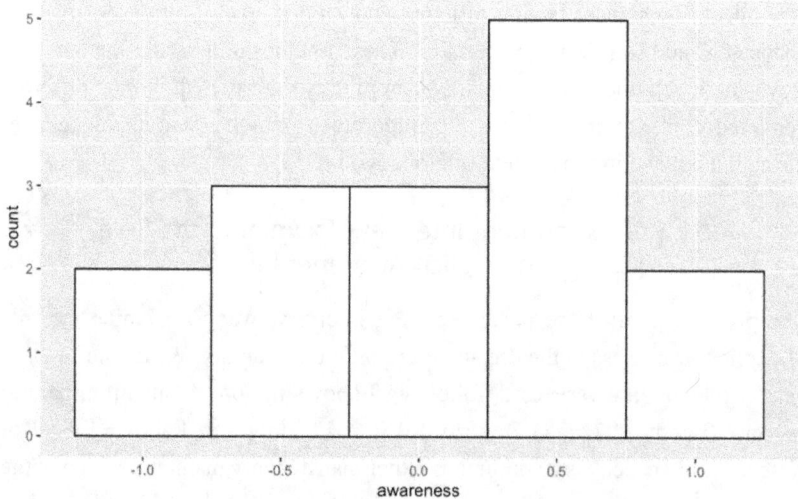

Figure 6 Distribution of awareness index values.

Table 5 Comparison of actual and perceived frequency of uptalk usage, and relationship with derived "awareness" variable

name	gender	% of actual [+ uptalk] use (raw)	actual use (scaled to 1-3)	actual use (coded as categorical)[3]	perceived use (raw)	perceived use (scaled to 1 to 3)	difference between actual use and perceived use (degree of over-rating)	absolute difference (un-scaled awareness)	awareness index
Mason	M	0.61	1.00	seldom	seldom	1.00	0.00	0.00	1.00
Maya	F	32.83	3.00	often	often	3.00	0.00	0.00	1.00
Johnson	M	4.64	1.25	sometimes	seldom	1.00	-0.25	0.25	0.72
Yasmin	F	22.57	2.36	sometimes	sometimes	2.00	-0.36	0.36	0.59
Levi	M	9.91	1.58	sometimes	sometimes	2.00	0.42	0.42	0.53
Gabriella	F	23.53	2.42	often	sometimes	2.00	-0.42	0.42	0.53
Tamara	F	8.23	1.47	sometimes	sometimes	2.00	0.53	0.53	0.41
Cecilia	F	12.07	1.71	sometimes	often	3.00	-0.71	0.71	0.20
Emery	M	3.82	1.20	seldom	sometimes	2.00	0.80	0.80	0.10
Hayley	F	15.42	1.92	sometimes	often	3.00	1.08	1.08	-0.21
George	M	19.78	2.19	sometimes	seldom	1.00	-1.19	1.19	-0.34
Tyler	M	11.76	1.69	sometimes	often	3.00	1.31	1.31	-0.47
Gia	F	11.44	1.67	sometimes	often	3.00	1.33	1.33	-0.49
Samuel	M	26.78	2.62	often	seldom	1.00	-1.62	1.62	-0.82
Theodora	F	4.15	1.22	seldom	often	3.00	1.78	1.78	-1.00

[3] To ensure the comparability of the results with the variable "perceived use," the continuous variable of "actual use" was recoded based on standard deviation intervals from the mean. Scores falling within ±1 standard deviation from the mean were categorized as "sometimes." Scores within +2 to +3 standard deviations from the mean were categorized as "often," while scores within −2 to −3 standard deviations from the mean were categorized as "seldom."

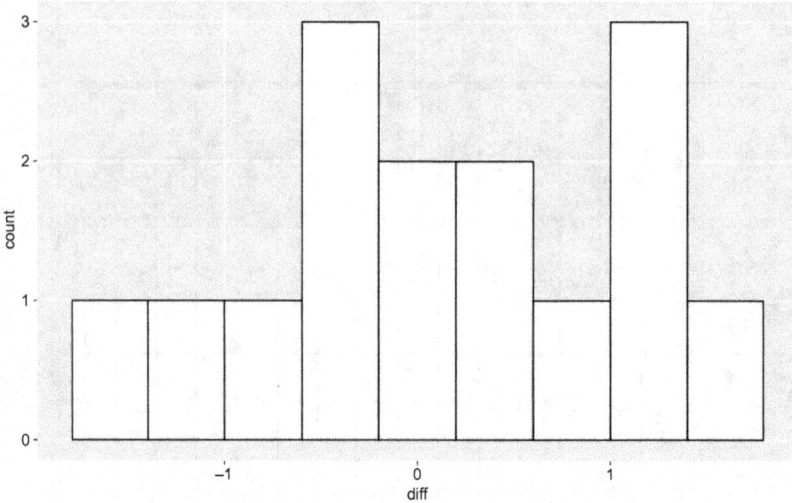

Figure 7 Distribution of degrees of overrating.

(mean = 0.12, standard error = 0.17, median = 0.2), suggesting a prevalent awareness of uptalk usage among most participants. Nonetheless, there is significant variability ($SD = 0.64$, kurtosis = -1.37) in the dataset. The negative kurtosis suggests that awareness levels are more spread out than in a normal distribution. This means that compared to a normal distribution's outliers, there are more extreme cases – both individuals with very high awareness and those with very low awareness. This dispersion from the center reflects greater variability in how aware people are of uptalk usage. Given its placement on Labov's (1972a) continuum of sociolinguistic variables, which ranges from indicators to markers and stereotypes, uptalk's awareness distribution may – given the evidence that we currently have at this point – position it closer to a marker, where some degree of social awareness is evident but does not yet reach the explicit recognition of a stereotype. Speakers seem to be aware of uptalk to some extent, but they do explicitly and fully control it in the way they do with explicit stereotypes.

Focusing solely on one measure of awareness – how frequently participants overestimate their uptalk usage compared to their actual usage – shows considerable variability (Figure 7). This variability is evident, with some participants overestimating their uptalk usage. The spread in the distribution is further evidenced by the kurtosis and standard deviation values (kurtosis = -1.12, $SD = 0.98$), indicating a broad range of responses. Figure 7 also illustrates that the distribution is not statistically normal (i.e., not like a normal, bell-curved distribution). A holistic analysis of the data, considering the overall average (mean = 0.18, $SD = 0.98$), suggests that participants tend to slightly

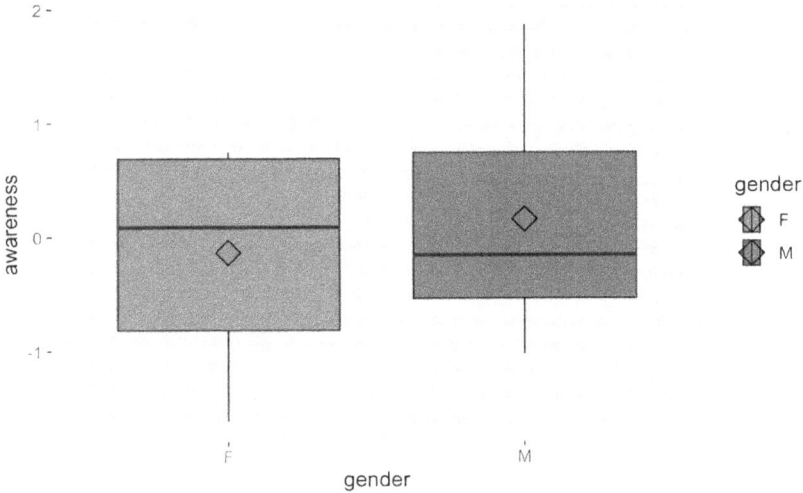

Figure 8 Distribution of awareness by gender.

overestimate their uptalk usage during the production experiment. Nonetheless, there is a significant dispersion in how much participants overrate or overestimate their uptalk usage. This again aligns with Labov's categorization of markers – linguistic variables that speakers may be variably aware of, depending on social exposure and context. The evidence up to this point suggests that uptalk remains a marker rather than a fully realized stereotype.

Given that gender has been found to be a robust predictor of sociolinguistic variation, a question emerges: Are HKE-speaking women in our sample more likely to be aware of uptalk use? And what can it potentially say about the stability of the uptalk variable? Our results show some gender differences in awareness of uptalk (Figure 8). Generally, if one looks at the medians (more appropriate for our non-normally distributed data), we have evidence that female participants (median = 0.10, $n = 8$) demonstrate greater awareness of uptalk than male participants (median = −0.19, $n = 7$).

This finding aligns with Labov's predictions about stable variation, which suggest that when a linguistic variable remains stable over time rather than undergoing change, women tend to exhibit greater awareness of its usage and social implications. For example, in English, the alternation between *-ing* (as in *walking*) and *-in'* (as in *walkin'*) has been identified as a stable sociolinguistic variable, with research showing that women are more likely to use the standard *-ing* form and to be explicitly aware of its social significance (Meyerhoff 2018). Similarly, the gender difference in uptalk awareness may indicate that uptalk is not undergoing change but is instead a stable feature of HKE.

Figure 9 Distribution of tendency to overrate uptalk usage by gender.

Concentrating once more on a specific indicator of awareness – the frequency with which participants overestimate their use of uptalk, based on the actual differences between their perceived and actual uptalk usage – we observe more pronounced gender differences (Figure 9). In general, our female listeners (mean = 0.403, SD = 0.91, n = 8) are more prone to overestimating their uptalk usage compared to male listeners (mean = −0.08, SD = 1.04, n = 7). Female participants in the interviews are more likely to claim they use uptalk more than they actually do, in contrast to male participants.

One possible explanation for this overestimation is that while they associate uptalk with hesitancy in others' speech, they may perceive their own use as strategic rather than uncertain. This aligns with our evidence in Figure 5 that uptalk can also signal confidence or ease, not merely hesitation. Social desirability effects likely contribute to this overestimation, as uptalk is linked to politeness and femininity in English-speaking contexts (Tyler 2015), leading women to report usage in accordance with perceived social norms. Eckert (1989) further contextualizes this overestimation, arguing that gender-based linguistic variation reflects social constructs and power dynamics rather than biological sex alone. With historically limited institutional power, women have relied more on symbolic capital, including linguistic resources, to assert identity and navigate social hierarchies. Thus their overestimation may not stem from interpreting their own uptalk as hesitant but from drawing on alternative social meanings or aligning with communicative strategies expected of/imposed on their gender.

A key contextual factor is that all participants are university students, likely exposed to academic discourse on HRT or uptalk and its gendered associations. This awareness may shape self-perceptions, particularly among women, who may feel greater pressure to conform to or resist these expectations. If uptalk is saliently linked to femininity, women may internalize its use as part of their identity while simultaneously critiquing or downplaying it in others. Their overestimation may therefore reflect gendered ideologies rather than actual speech patterns acquired from university socialization.

These findings must be reconciled with earlier evidence positioning uptalk as a socially meaningful marker in the Labovian sense – neither entirely below explicit awareness nor fully enregistered as a stereotype. The observed gender-based differences in awareness suggest that uptalk in HKE occupies a fluid space on the sociolinguistic continuum. While overestimation among female participants points to its potential emergence as a stereotype, variability in awareness mitigates this. The following section explores this further by examining participants' perceptions of uptalk's social meanings.

5.2.2 Evaluations of [+ Uptalk] above the Level of Awareness

In this section, we aim to identify the meanings listeners assign to uptalk when it is explicitly highlighted. We concentrate solely on the evaluations of [+ uptalk] to maintain focus. To guarantee comparability, we used the same participants as in the evaluation experiment. We start with a qualitative analysis of the word clouds produced and complement this analysis with a thematic content analysis of the interviews to deepen our understanding of the variable and its association with gender and other social meanings.

Word Cloud Comparison

Examining the explicit evaluations collectively, the most prevalent perception of [+ uptalk] is a lack of confidence (Figure 10), followed by other notable but less common evaluations such as [+ uptalk] being associated with "women"/"females," "uncertain," and "emotional," along with perceptions of a lack of education and professionalism, and descriptors like "careful," "young," "inauthentic," "uncomfortable," "expressive," "queer," and "comedic."

When compared to implicit evaluations, some similarities emerge: Both levels of awareness prominently associate uptalk with a lack of confidence. Other less frequent descriptions common to explicit and implicit evaluations include uncertainty, women/female, inauthenticity, youth, and deficiencies in English proficiency and professionalism. Descriptors distinctly prominent in implicit evaluations that are not emphasized in explicit evaluations include

Figure 10 Summary of explicit evaluations of [+ uptalk] overall (word cloud).

hesitancy, being educated, less aggressiveness, and local Hong Kong identity. On the other hand, traits prominently noted in explicit evaluations but absent in implicit evaluations include queerness, discomfort, expressiveness, lack of education, humor, and carefulness.

The comparative analysis demonstrates that while both explicit and implicit evaluations of uptalk share a foundational set of semi-static meanings, the salience and activation of specific social meanings are influenced by the degree of explicit awareness. Notably, in relation to the association of uptalk with "women" and "females," our findings indicate that individuals who are explicitly aware of the variable are more likely to foreground these meanings than when they are not. This suggests that uptalk's status as a stereotype is contingent on awareness: When explicitly evaluated, it operates closer to a stereotype, whereas in the absence of such awareness, it functions more as a sociolinguistic marker. More broadly, these findings point to the role of awareness in shaping the activation and modulation of social meanings associated with uptalk in HKE.

A comparison of explicit evaluations of uptalk between male and female listeners shows distinct differences (Figure 11). When explicitly asked to evaluate [+ uptalk], most male listeners primarily associate uptalk with women. Interestingly, both groups do not link uptalk with "femininity," as it was not mentioned during the data collection. A visual examination of the word clouds from male evaluations reveals other associated meanings, although they are less prevalent than "women." These include queerness (e.g., "LGBTQ"), lack of English proficiency, uncertainty, humor, inauthenticity, expressiveness, outgoingness, and lack of confidence. This provides evidence that speakers attribute various meanings to the use of uptalk, extending beyond merely explicit gender-related meanings.

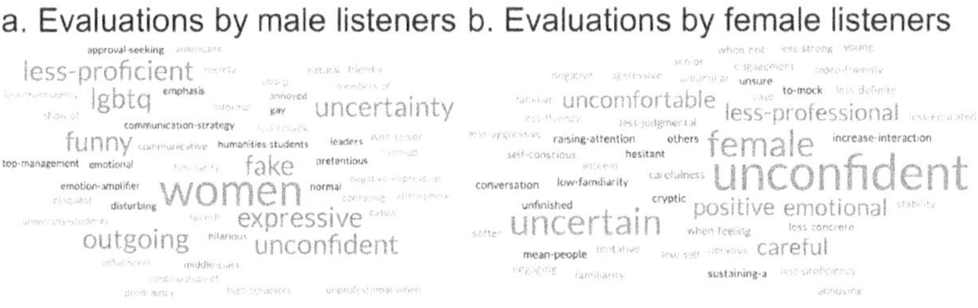

a. Evaluations by male listeners b. Evaluations by female listeners

Figure 11 Summary of explicit evaluations of uptalk by gender of listener (word cloud).

Comparing this with evaluations by female listeners shows that "women" or "female" is not the primary social evaluation; instead, it is a lack of confidence. This is followed by evaluations related to uncertainty and women. Notably, when making gendered evaluations, female listeners tend to use the term "female," in contrast to male listeners, who tend to use "women." Beyond uncertainty and meanings of "women," female listeners also tend to perceive uptalk as indicating discomfort, lesser professionalism, carefulness, positivity, and emotionality.

Worth noting is that in both cases of explicitly evaluating uptalk among male and female listeners, "woman" can be analyzed as a central theme, as the evaluations comprise direct indexes of womanhood and being female (e.g., "women", "female") as well as indirect meanings that can be ideologically linked to these (e.g., "emotional"). The main distinction lies in the specific descriptors used. In the case of male listeners, a stereotypical kind of womanhood and being female seems to be indirectly indexed through the use of descriptors such as "unconfident," "approval-seeking," "eloquent," and "emotional," whereas in the case of female listeners, this femininity seems to be indirectly indexed by terms such as "emotional," "careful," "hesitant," "cryptic," and "soft."

If we compare explicit evaluations of uptalk with implicit ones by listener gender, notable differences emerge. For male listeners, less explicit awareness of uptalk seems to encourage associations with localness and educatedness, alongside a lack of confidence. However, once uptalk is explicitly recognized and male listeners become aware of the variable, these meanings recede, making way for associations predominantly with "woman." In fact, local Hong Kong-ness and educatedness almost completely give way to womanhood, queerness, inauthenticity, lack of proficiency, and humor, among other meanings. On the other hand, female listeners, when implicitly aware of uptalk, associate it with hesitancy, educatedness, some American-ness, uncertainty, and informality. Yet when these listeners are explicitly aware of uptalk, they describe it as "womanlike," "positive," "emotional," "careful," "less professional," and "uncomfortable." Certain implicit associations like "American," "well-spoken," and class-based interpretations of uptalk vanish in explicit evaluations. This underscores that awareness plays at least some role in mediating the relationship between [+ uptalk] and its indexical values.

A clear trend emerges showing that while gendered meanings and indexicals underlie implicit evaluations among listeners, this is particularly notable among male listeners, some of whom directly link [+ uptalk] with femininity. This inclination toward feminine evaluations intensifies with heightened awareness: After becoming explicitly aware of the variable, most male listeners now primarily associate uptalk with womanhood. Conversely, female listeners, who did not link uptalk with womanhood in their implicit evaluations prominently mention womanhood as an indexical of uptalk when made explicitly aware of it. These "female" evaluations by female listeners are significantly present, though they are overshadowed by the more dominant evaluation of "lack of confidence" – a contrast to male listeners, who mostly tie uptalk to womanhood.

Thematic Content Analysis of Interviews

Recognizing that comparing keywords extracted during the interview may not offer us the whole picture of explicit social meanings related to uptalk, we conducted a thematic content analysis of all interviews. In the interest of conciseness, we report only prominent themes that emerged during the interview.

Linking of Uptalk to Womanhood: From Indirect to Direct?

The first theme confirms what we suspected in the word cloud analysis – uptalk is not always directly linked to gender. In the analysis, terms related to womanhood and female-ness were more prevalent in interview contexts (explicit evaluation) than in the evaluation experiment (implicit evaluation). Further examination of the interviews indicated that women-related descriptors are used more often because listeners frequently make gender-based ideological associations between uptalk and traits they associate with womanhood. We frequently observed indexical chains where uptalk is connected to potentially gendered traits or descriptors, which in turn are linked to a specific type of womanhood. Specifically, it appears that listeners use a top-down logic when discussing uptalk; they assert that women display certain essentialized gendered traits, leading to their use of uptalk. First, they expressed that women are less confident than men and are therefore more likely to use uptalk to show hesitation. Second, they remarked that women are more sentimental and emotional than men, and thus use uptalk to vary the tone and add emotions to the plain declarative sentence. Third, they believed that women are more willing to maintain discourse continuity than men, thus the use of uptalk shows their wish to gain some agreement or response from the audience. This ideological link, where gender and stereotypes are viewed as causes for uptalk usage, likely did not originate from these reasons, nor does it reflect women's inherent characteristics, but rather social meanings perceived as womanlike.

More Than "Women's Speech": The Role of Intersectionality

Another theme that emerged from our interview analysis is that references to womanhood are not always made in isolation. While they could be, we observed instances where participants invoked intersectional identities in their discussions of uptalk, instead of simply labeling it as a "woman" or "female" trait. Within our group of participants, five individuals – two males and three females, representing 33% of our sample – explicitly linked uptalk to femininity. Additionally, two participants, one male and one female, pointed out that young women, particularly those in high school and university, tend to use uptalk (4). This observation suggests that listeners do not solely associate uptalk with gender; they also relate it to other social dimensions such as age, educational level, and independence.

(4) *"[Uptalk]'s sort of entrenched in ... young females ... high schoolers, maybe university students do tend to use uptalk a lot more than, you know, more mature people."* (Emery)

It could even be argued that in our context, uptalk is tied to complex intersectional gendered identities (e.g., femininities) that are constituted by personae like the "nerd school girl," depicted as educated and young (Bucholtz 1999), and perhaps the "Kong Girl" persona (Kang & Chen 2017), which shares attributes of youth, femininity, and independence with the "university/high school female student" social type identified by participants. Notably, none of our interviewees explicitly linked uptalk with masculinity.

Uptalk, Confidence, and Stance-Taking

The discussion around uptalk does not always involve gender. In fact, throughout the interviews, many participants did not mention gender at all, even when explicitly prompted about the UPTALK variable. A prominent theme identified was the association of uptalk with a lack of confidence (5 to 8). Almost all participants (four males and eight females) linked uptalk to uncertainty. They observed that the rising intonation at the end of a declarative sentence often makes it sound like a question, which can suggest to listeners that the speaker is unsure of their statements, not well versed in the topic, less fluent in English, or trying to convey a lower social status, such as a worker addressing a superior. In essence, the use of rising intonation in uptalk is interpreted by attentive listeners as indicating a hesitant or unconfident stance (Kiesling 2005; Du Bois 2007), or as a sign of deference, a common politeness strategy in East Asian cultures, including Hong Kong.

(5) *"I think mostly when I'm not familiar with the topic or maybe when I'm nervous I might naturally use **uptalk** ... when I'm uncertain or when I'm hesitating or thinking about like what I'm going to talk about so I think that's quite natural for people to or me personally to like to **raise my tone** as like a question to or maybe express my uncertainty."* (Hayley)

(6) *"I tend to use it* **[uptalk]** *like when I'm unsure about my answer."* (Tamara)

(7) *I think this one was also ... I think it was a bit ... less confident than the third speaker because maybe at the end, there was also like a **raise in the tone** at the end and that made him sound quite ... rushed* (Tyler)

(8) *For the uncertainty, I guess that through her intonation ... the **pitch rises** when when she, at the end of the sentence* (Gabriella)

It is worth noting that not all participants associated the use of uptalk with low confidence. One male participant suggested an association between uptalk and high confidence. He believed that uptalk could index a stance of confidence through demonstration of a higher English proficiency, stronger social skills, and an outgoing, friendly personality. Although he does not directly mention this, his descriptions seem to be associated with the preppy "cosmopolitan (male) foreigner" social type in Hong Kong, which we have discussed briefly in Section 5.1.2. The difference between the findings of this section and Section 5.1.2 is that, in that section, the social type was implicitly linked to men's nonuse of uptalk. However, of note in this section, when made explicit of the variable uptalk, it was uptalk and not nonuse of uptalk that was linked to this preppy social type. This suggests that explicit awareness plays at least some role in moderating the link between linguistic variables, social meanings, stance-taking, and gendered personae. The findings provide further evidence that indeed social meanings only emerge in social context (Hall-Lew, Moore, & Podesva 2021).

Uptalk and English Proficiency

One theme that we did not expect to surface in the interviews was explicit linking of uptalk to English proficiency. Several participants – two males and three females – suggested that uptalk might indicate lower English proficiency. They argued that since English is a foreign language in Hong Kong, one may be less fluent in speaking English and need more time to think while speaking. The lack of confidence in their English level and the need to slow down their speech motivated their use of uptalk. Worth noting here is that participants did not just refer to English proficiency when talking about the meaning of uptalk. They also invoked notions of lack of confidence. An ideological linking between lack of confidence and lack of English "proficiency" is being made here, where the participants, holding standard language ideologies that are highly prevalent in an ex-British colony, Hong Kong, assumed an inherent essential link between "good" and "proficient" English with English that is "fast," "fluent," and "confident" (9 and 10). These findings highlight the complex and interrelated social meanings associated with uptalk. Rather than simply viewing uptalk as indicative of either a lack of confidence or limited English proficiency, it is crucial to recognize that these factors might be ideologically linked or clustered locally, as seen in this instance.

(9) *"I'm not proficient in English and my mother language is also not English. So sometimes I cannot speak fluently so I might try to speak slowly so may ... the last word may feel like **uptalk**. So it feels like a question. So ... it's like ... speaking, like, not confidently."* (Maya)

The complexities of uptalk extend even further, as it is not necessarily always ideologically linked to a lack of confidence. One participant specifically pointed out that uptalk could signify high English proficiency, suggesting that uptalk makes the speech sound more natural and native-like, as opposed to flat and monotonous. Upon closer examination, this view also relates to confidence – specifically, high confidence. How can we explain such varied interpretations and sociolinguistic patterns? We argue that these differences stem from how two aspects of uptalk are interpreted: the rising intonation and the dynamic, non-monotonous pitch,[4] and which aspect of uptalk is being paid attention to. Evidence from our interviews shows that the rising intonation is often associated with question-asking, which is then linked to uncertainty, a lack of confidence, and insufficient English proficiency.

---

[4] While declarative sentences exhibit pitch declination rather than true monotony, our findings suggest that participants perceived the absence of uptalk as "stable" intonation. This likely reflects the contrast between uptalk's dynamic pitch movement and the smoother contour of nonuptalk speech. As one participant noted: *"Maybe during work I **won't use uptalk**, because during work you have to be like very professional, so you have to maintain very **stable** ... **stable** ... **intonation**."* This suggests that when participants describe speech as lacking uptalk, they overlook natural pitch declination in favor of perceived tonal stability.

(10) *I use **uptalk** quite a lot because when I because I'm **not a proficiency in English** and my mother language is also not English. So sometimes I cannot speak fluently so I may try to speak slowly so may ... the last word may feel like uptalk. So it's like ... I **feel like a question**. So it's maybe it seems like it's like speaking like not confidently. So most of the time it's like in a discussion especially because you are not confident with what you just point out, or your statement. So maybe we state like **uptalking uptone** [rising tone]*. (Maya)

In contrast, the nonmonotonous, varied tone of uptalk was identified by participants and associated with higher English proficiency. This is particularly evident in Mason's reflection, where he attributes his difficulty in perceiving or producing such tonal dynamism – what he refers to as "emotional variability" – to his "bad" intonation and limited English skills, as illustrated in his remarks: "I don't speak English," "I don't know, varying ...," as seen in the example (11). This suggests that the use of higher tonal dynamism is linked to notions of nativeness and proficiency in English in HKE.

(11) *I **don't speak English** so often ..., there **is little** ... I **don't know, varying**, you know, like it varies from different situation ... And my **intonation is quite bad**. So I don't have emotion in my English ... actually. So maybe that's why I **can't hear** those, you know, the emotional characteristic or something of those four recordings*. (Mason)

From this, we outline two distinct "routes" that [+ uptalk] can take, leading to these contrasting interpretations:

1. [+ uptalk] > rising tone > question-like > lack of confidence = lack of proficiency in English
2. [+ uptalk] > nonmonotonous tone > natural/native-like > proficiency in English > high confidence

Uptalk and Sociability: Politeness, Stance and Affect

Another theme that emerged from the interviews, which is not specifically tied to gender, is the use of uptalk as a means to establish or seek connections with others, a concept we operationalize as "sociability." We describe sociability as the ability to interact comfortably with others, encompassing qualities such as politeness, friendliness, approachability, and a preference for group activities. This theme underscores the role of uptalk in facilitating easy communication within social settings.

We found that participants use uptalk to promote smoother and more polite interactions, enhancing their "sociability." Many participants (four males and two females) specifically noted that an utterance with uptalk sounds softer, friendlier, and less confrontational than a typical declarative sentence, particularly when making judgments or criticisms or challenging ideas. This is salient in Emery and Samuel's comment.

(12) *But intonation-wise, I ... I did hear some sort of **uprising tone** which I think indicates ... I don't know, how should I put it, sort of ease, I don't know, sort of like a sense of **ease when talking.*** (Emery)

(13) *I'm having this kind of **tone rising** or you know I don't know whether it is a tone or a prosody but yeah let us put it a tone first and yeah, you know having this kind of tone **rising** or you know, a **very drastic turn of the tone.** It would be, would deliver a kind of, hilari ... I mean **hilarious** effect.* (Samuel)

In stark contrast, a plain declarative sentence in these contexts could come across as quite aggressive. According to participants, uptalk mitigates this harshness by indicating that the speaker's judgments, criticisms, or challenges are tentative (14). This is achieved by recasting the declarative as a pseudo-interrogative (15), effectively questioning oneself and indirectly prompting listeners to respond. This framing positions the statement as a suggestion rather than a directive, which respects individuals' desire for autonomy and freedom from imposition – key aspects of negative politeness (Brown & Levinson 1987). Thus, even though "politeness" was not directly cited as a meaning of uptalk during the interviews, participants indirectly engaged with this concept. Consequently, in the context of East Asian cultures like Hong Kong, where negative politeness is highly valued, using uptalk is also perceived as a polite communication strategy.

(14) *"Maybe they care about how people think about what they say, how people would react to their statements. So they may add some **uptalks** to their conversation to make it sounds less concrete or sounds ... sounds less sure, **less judgmental**."* (Theodora)

(15) *"If you use ... uptalk, that sounds like you have some questions and you want others to help you or give you some more elaboration."* (Tyler)

The theme of uptalk indexing sociability was further evident when participants described how an utterance with uptalk can make interactions more engaging and interactive in two ways. First, participants identified uptalk as a method to encourage audience engagement and reaction. For instance, one participant observed that a speaker might use uptalk to express hesitation or to adopt a tentative stance on their own statements, thereby inviting listeners' agreement, opinions, or advice (i.e., a stance of inquisitiveness) (14). This can be interpreted as the uptalk users having an open attitude or having an overall inclusive stance, which participants found to make a conversation more engaging compared to speakers who adopt a less inclusive distance stance through the nonuse of declaratives that can be interpreted as exclusive and noncompromising, and as such, less sociable.

Second, the use of uptalk was pointed out to "color" utterance with some kind of perceived affect that can ultimately be perceived as sociable. By affect, we refer to indexical cues in a broader stylistic landscape that includes attitudes, moods, and emotions (Pratt 2021). The concept here is that uptalk can evoke specific attitudes and emotions, or "affective qualities," such as enthusiasm or anger. This was supported by evidence from the interviews, where participants specifically noted that incorporating tonal variation into a monotone declarative utterance (i.e., uptalk) could express the speaker's strong emotions about the topic at hand:

(16) *I think it bases on their emotions. When their emotions have some **variations**, they will use this **tone** to say something, to talk with someone. Yeah, but yeah, I think this situation is why they would use this **tone [uptalk]**.* (Levi)

They explicitly noted that since uptalk can make a speech more emotive, attention-grabbing, and powerful, leaders and political figures are likely to use it. Here, participants made connections between the linguistic variable, social types, and affect: The affective qualities of a given social type are explicitly claimed to be reflected and enacted via sociolinguistic signs (and, of course, nonlinguistic signs), as when the "leader" or "political figure" social type is performed using uptalk, alongside its "powerful," "intense," and "enthusiastic" affect. This is evidenced in explicit comments such as this:

(17) *Maybe in working situations, **a leader** maybe like to use this **tones** [uptalk] ... I think it's necessary since he need to make something ... his talk **powerful**. Not just like, oh, today we need to do something.* (Levi)

Now, the social type and their associated meanings and affective qualities described by our participants could be seen in two different lights. On one hand, individuals embodying the quality of being a "leader" who use uptalk might be viewed as sociable. Such users of uptalk project an image of a "leader" who aims to be friendly, interactive, charismatic, convincing, polite, and articulate. On the other hand, the same use of uptalk could also conjure the image of an eager and uptight politician. While eagerness and uptightness were not explicitly mentioned in the interviews, the affective qualities discussed earlier – intense, enthusiastic, emotional, high energy – could also be interpreted as contributing to a broader sense of "dis-ease" or discomfort (Kiesling 2018), reflecting a "high-investment" stance perceived by listeners in those adopting a leadership role through their use of uptalk.

(18) *In workplace, I think if people use a lot of uptalk, then I think it may not be that professional, especially for doctors, nurses or social workers, etc. because **uptalk** sometimes for me is ... like has a **correlation with emotions**. Like they ... the frequency of using uptalk has a correlation with emotions. So being **too emotional** in a professional setting may **sound unprofessional** and that's why you may ...* (Yasmin)

When these speakers employ uptalk (and the entwined affective qualities), they might give the impression of being overly invested in their engagement, leading listeners to see them as less relaxed and not "at ease" (Kiesling 2018), and perhaps even less conventionally "masculine," as the traits of relaxation and calm have been ideologically linked to certain (hegemonic) masculinities (Kiesling 2018).

Interestingly, our data show evidence of both interpretations through an examination of metalinguistic comments – namely, the interpretation of "ease" or "sociability" and "dis-ease" or "lack of sociability" (i.e., being uptight or overeager). Some participants explicitly associated "leaders" and "politicians" with sociability in a positive light, as seen in direct mentions of being "more convincing," "less assertive," and "thoughtful" or "car[ing] [for] others' thoughts." However, other participants indicated that the use of uptalk can emphasize hierarchical distinctions and the subordinate position of listeners, creating a sense of discomfort and what we interpret as reduced sociability associated with uptalk. This is evidenced by direct mentions of "uncomfortable" during the interview.

Uptalk, Social Distance, and Familiarity

Closely related to the concept of sociability are social distance and familiarity, as we hinted in the previous section. From our analysis of the interview data, we observed that participants frequently suggested that the use of uptalk indicates a lack of familiarity. Nearly half of the participants mentioned that speakers are less likely to use uptalk with close friends and family for two main reasons: First, using uptalk with close contacts might imply that the speaker feels insecure or uncomfortable sharing their thoughts openly with them. Second, for about 30% of participants (three males and two females), uptalk is seen as a marker of doubt and ambiguity, potentially obscuring the speaker's true thoughts and emotions. This could be perceived as an act of social distancing, signaling emotional distance inappropriate for conversations with familiar listeners. Two female participants specifically noted that uptalk is more appropriate when speaking with unfamiliar people or strangers (19), as it avoids the "distancing" effect felt by close peers or family and instead sounds softer and less confrontational. Conversely, two participants provided opposing views, arguing that uptalk is better used with familiar individuals like close friends and family. They believe that uptalk is interpreted by these listeners as more emotional and expressive, thereby demonstrating the speaker's strong emotions, interest, and investment in the conversation.

(19) *"I also use uptalk when I'm talking to a stranger. Because I don't want to come off as offensive. It feels like a bit more friendly and nonaggressive."* (Gabriella)

What could explain the varied explicit evaluations of uptalk? Why is it interpreted as both "familiar" and "unfamiliar," capable of both bridging and widening the social distance between speakers? Following our previous discussion on proficiency, and although we lack psycholinguistic evidence at this point, our analysis of the interview data suggests that these discrepancies might be due to the different aspects of uptalk to which participants pay attention. Those who associate uptalk with familiarity and reducing social distance might focus more on the expressive range of pitch that uptalk can involve. From our interviews, this variation in pitch is linked to heightened emotionality and expressiveness, which in turn relates to notions of interest, investment, familiarity, and decreased social distance. In contrast, for participants who perceive uptalk as increasing social distance and signaling unfamiliarity, the focus seems to be on the rising pitch, often referred to in comments as the "[rising] tone" (20). This characteristic is commonly associated with questioning and doubt. Doubt, in turn, is linked to ambiguity and subsequently to inaccessibility (21), ultimately being interpreted as signaling unfamiliarity and greater social distance. We outline these divergent paths to understanding the social meanings of uptalk next:

1. [+ uptalk] > rising pitch > questions > doubt > ambiguity > inaccessibility > unfamiliarity, more social distance
2. [+ uptalk] > varied range of pitch > emotional, expressive > interest, investment > familiarity, less social distance

(20) *"If that people use too much [of] this [rising] tone ... to talk to me, I think I can't feel their heart ... I think it is acting."* (Levi)

(21) *"It is not easy to get into their heart or their mind. And it acts like a wall building between us, a border between us."* (Johnson)

Overall, our findings reveal mixed evaluations of uptalk in terms of familiarity, a theme that prominently emerged in our qualitative analysis. Some participants viewed uptalk as unfamiliar and a means to increase social distance, suggesting it should be avoided with familiar peers or family. Conversely, others saw it as familiar and a tool to decrease social distance, useful for engaging strangers and appearing more friendly. Our in-depth analysis suggests that these differing interpretations may stem from where listeners focus their attention on specific aspects of uptalk. This attention could shape the social meanings and values assigned to uptalk. In essence, how listeners attend to components of uptalk seems to influence how its use is connected to notions of familiarity, essentially moderating the relationship between uptalk and familiarity perceptions.

In Section 5.3, some of these qualitative trends will be cross-examined with our quantitative findings, which will shed light on the actual usage of uptalk and their correlations with the connotations of uptalk.

5.3 Quantitative Findings: Production Experiment

5.3.1 Overview

In this section, we report the outcomes of our quantitative investigation. Initially, we introduce the findings of our Bayesian regression analysis, identifying the factors with a significant likelihood of influencing the use of UPTALK. Subsequent to establishing the robustness of our model through rigorous evaluations, we pinpoint and discuss the factors that prominently condition UPTALK, then rank them according to their predictive power based on results from the Boruta algorithm analysis. Given the nuanced interplay of gender with other sociolinguistic variables – highlighted in both our qualitative insights and current scholarly discourse – we further examine how these variables intersect with gender, assessing the potential of UPTALK to construct complex social identities (e.g., young woman, female Hong Konger). Last, informed by our earlier qualitative analysis that highlighted awareness as a moderator of UPTALK evaluation and, consequently, the social meanings of UPTALK, we examine the role of speaker awareness in conditioning the impact of these social factors on UPTALK usage, thereby seeking to validate the qualitative dimensions of our research.

5.3.2 The Bayesian Model: Overview and Evaluation

The statistical modeling results indicate that among the forty-six factors considered in the analysis, including interaction effects and the random intercept factors "participant" and "conversation pair," approximately 41% ($n = 19$) are strongly associated ($pd > 0.70$) with UPTALK (see supplementary resources). These factors include type of utterance, sentiment, gender context, conversation pair, and interaction between speaker gender and gender context, as well as individual characteristics. We discuss all robust factors for predicting uptalk (non)use beginning in Section 5.3.3. To assist in interpreting the results of our Bayesian model, which we will discuss in the following section, we have included the frequency distribution of uptalk variants by variable in the supplementary resources.

5.3.3 Factors That Are Likely to Condition UPTALK

Among the factors not involving interaction, seven were found to significantly condition the use of UPTALK.

Temporal Factor

First, the influence of time on uptalk usage is apparent in our results: Participants tended to use more uptalk at the beginning of their dyadic conversations. Based on the marginal means of our model – the means after taking into account all factors in the model – this usage seems to decrease as the conversations continue ($pd = 1$) (Figure 12).

This pattern might be connected to the concept of speech awareness (Bell 1984), where speakers, highly aware of being observed by both their conversation partners and facilitators, may use more uptalk due to nervousness or uncertainty, as a kind of defense mechanism to not sound too assertive and "lose face." As the conversation progresses, this awareness seems to have decreased, leading to a reduction in uptalk. However, as our findings show, the impact of time on uptalk usage is not consistent across individuals (Figure 13). Some participants decrease their use of uptalk, while others increase it as they become more familiar with the situation. These results indicate that uptalk is not merely a defensive mechanism or a means to convey politeness by avoiding assertiveness at the start. As suggested by earlier qualitative findings and our quantitative results, uptalk may also signal other nuances, such as a reduction in social distance or an increase in engagement or investment with the interlocutor, highlighting the multifaceted role of uptalk when considering the temporal dimension.

Interactional Factor: Conversation Pair

The interaction within conversation pairs or dyads emerges as another significant factor potentially affecting the variation in UPTALK. Some pairs exhibit higher uptalk rates, ranging from 4% to 27%, while others display lower rates (Figure 14). Identifying the specific reasons for increased uptalk within certain dyads is challenging due to the multitude of overlapping and interrelated factors. For instance, an individual's unique social identities and behaviors might lead to different interactional styles depending on their conversation partner.

Another evident source of interdyad variation in UPTALK rates is the subject matter or topic of the conversations. In our production experiment,

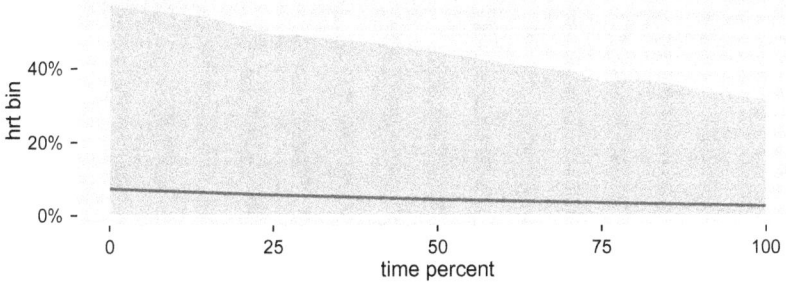

Figure 12 Marginal means: The effect of time on UPTALK use.

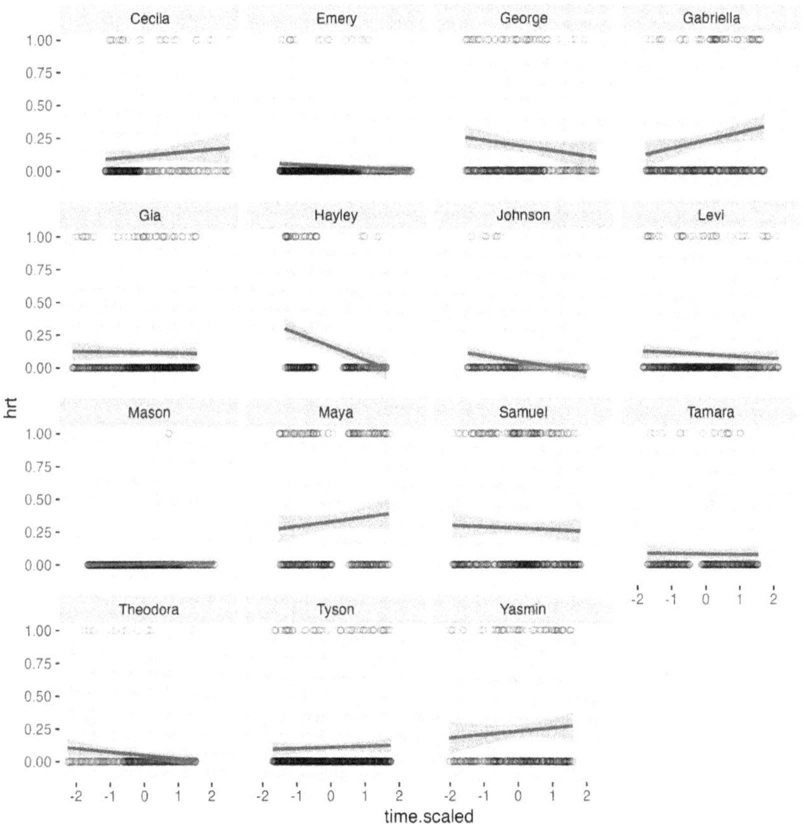

Figure 13 Marginal means: The effect of time on UPTALK use (by individual).

we allowed participant pairs to select their own discussion topics, which introduced a wide range of topics for analysis and highlighted differences in uptalk usage across different conversation pairs. Investigating the content of these discussions through topic modeling or latent Dirichlet allocation

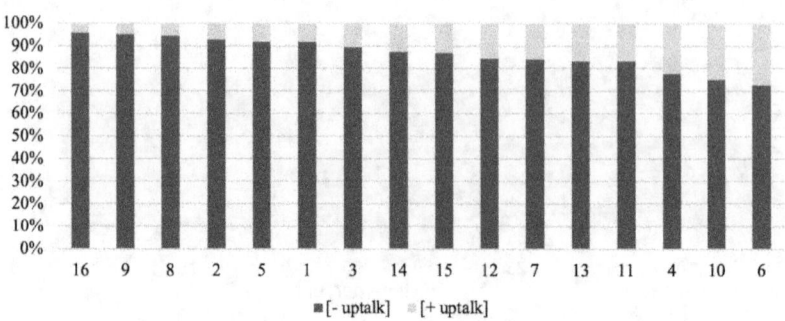

Figure 14 The effect of conversation pair/dyad on UPTALK use.

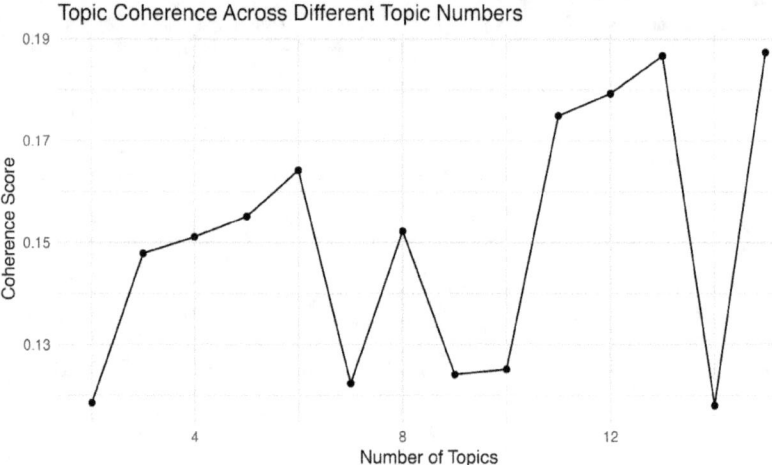

Figure 15 Topic coherence score (Cao et al. 2009) by number of topics.

(LDA) analysis (Blei, Ng, & Jordan 2003), which treats each conversation as a composition of various topics, can illuminate how different subjects affect uptalk usage. For instance, topics that are more personal could induce higher uptalk rates as speakers strive to engage their listeners and confirm comprehension or consensus. In contrast, topics that are more factual or informational could result in lower uptalk rates due to less need for engagement. The coherence scores from our LDA topic modeling analysis, following the approach of Cao et al. (2009), identified thirteen primary topics within our experiment (Figure 15), such as student lifestyle and challenges, social and recreational aspects of school life, and community and group dynamics in education. The full list of topics and related keywords can be found in the supplementary resources.

By analyzing the utterances from each conversation pair in terms of these topics, we observe significant variability (Figure 16). For example, the

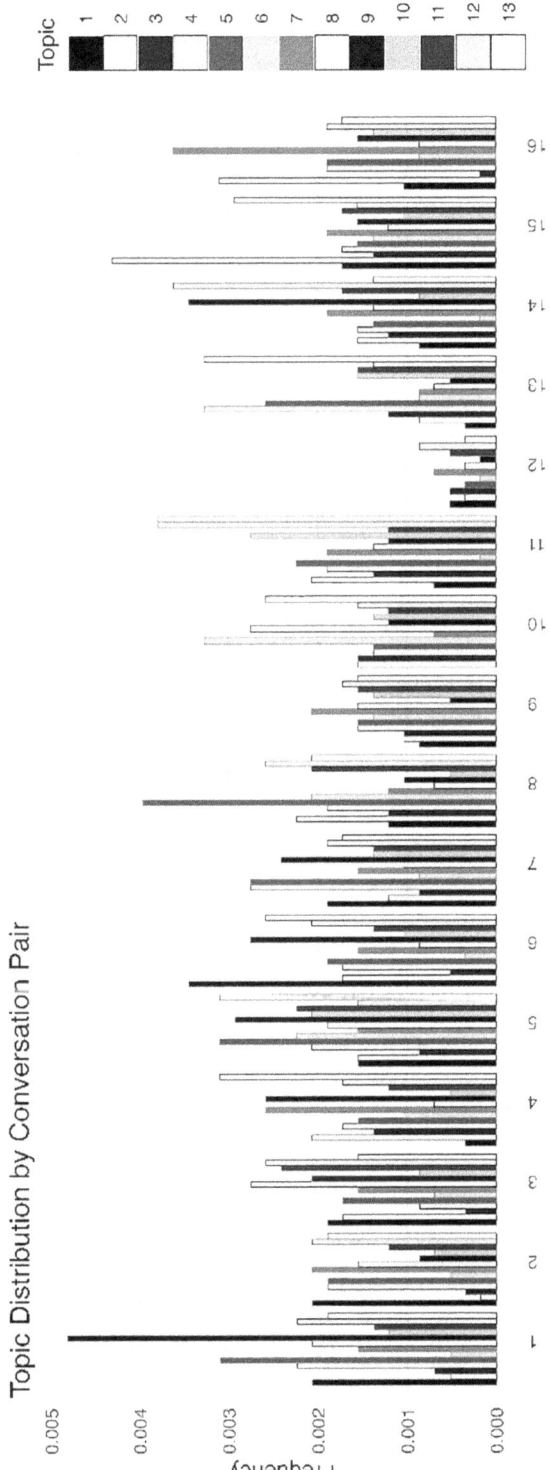

Figure 16 Topic distribution by conversation pair.

conversation of pair 1 is largely dominated by the topic "Learning Methods and Academic Support," while pair 8 focuses on "Graduation and Career Planning." Notably, the pairs with the highest uptalk rates – pairs 4, 6, and 10 – show a marked interest in topics such as "Personal Development and Self-Improvement" and, to a lesser extent, "Learning Methods and Academic Support." This pattern suggests that the relationship between conversation dynamics and uptalk usage might be significantly influenced by the choice of topics.

Age Factor

Although the likelihood is lower (pd = 0.6), age also appears as a contributing factor influencing uptalk usage. According to the marginal means, which isolate the effect of age from other confounding factors in the model, there is a higher-than-random probability that older participants (i.e., those in their early twenties) use more uptalk compared to younger participants (i.e., those who are nineteen and twenty years old). However, this effect is not as pronounced as those observed with "individual" or "conversation pair" factors. Nonetheless, the observation concerning age is intriguing, as it supports our earlier qualitative discovery that uptalk is linked to a specific gendered youth social type: the "young female university student" social type.

Factors Related to Gender

Interestingly, speaker gender does not exert a direct influence on UPTALK: The probability of direction (pd = 0.5) suggests minimal variation in uptalk patterns between female and male speakers. Preliminary analyses based on descriptive frequency suggested a higher incidence of uptalk among women; however, subsequent Bayesian regression adjusting for confounding variables negated this apparent gender effect. Both genders appear to deploy uptalk equivalently once other notable factors are controlled. This absence of a significant gender correlation with uptalk usage diverges from findings in Western sociolinguistic research, which often directly associates uptalk with femininity (Britain 1992; Slobe 2018). However, it aligns with our qualitative data, where we found that participants who are unaware of their uptalk usage did not explicitly associate it with femininity. The findings of our quantitative/production and qualitative analyses are comparable, as in the production task, participants were similarly likely to be unaware of their uptalk usage. Our qualitative findings earlier thus provide some support to our current quantitative finding that the gender of the speaker does not directly condition (implicit) uptalk production. They suggest that, in the context of Hong Kong and HKE, feminine meanings are not directly and invariably associated with uptalk – the gendered meanings of uptalk seem to be multilayered and contextual. Other factors such as the speaker's awareness of uptalk, as noted in our qualitative findings, may mediate the influence of speaker gender on uptalk usage, where greater levels of awareness of uptalk would increase the level of activation of the feminine meanings of uptalk. Furthermore, the departure from Western-centric interpretations challenges the notion that the direct association of uptalk with femininity is a universal linguistic phenomenon. Within the specific sociolinguistic environment of HKE, it appears that factors such as the dynamics of the conversational dyad and the nature of the utterance are more reliable direct predictors of uptalk usage than the gender of the speaker.

While speaker gender does not directly impact UPTALK, the gender context within the conversation does. Our results indicate that individuals in mixed-gender conversational settings are more likely to use uptalk than those in same-gender settings. This pattern is supported by our descriptive statistics and marginal means (Tables 5 and 7, $pd = 0.7$), demonstrating a clear difference in uptalk usage based on the gender composition of the conversational pairs. This finding can be interpreted as a manifestation of gender negotiation, where individuals deploy uptalk either to resist or align with the normative expectations held by interlocutors of the same or different gender. This interpretation is well supported, as our prior qualitative research indicates that uptalk is differentially evaluated and interpreted across gender lines, with male and female speakers and listeners holding distinct attitudes. These perceptions underscore a complex array of implicit and at times explicit normative expectations regarding gender-specific communicative behaviors. Such gendered expectations, irrespective of whether they originate from interlocutors of the same or different gender, exert a discernible influence on the deployment of uptalk by speakers.

We witness a similar effect of gender context or more specifically, gendered linguistic accommodation on uptalk use in Gratton's (2016) investigation into the use of the (ING) variable (e.g., *runnin'* vs. *running*) by transgender individuals in the greater Toronto area. Gratton's findings indicate that these individuals modulate their use of the (ING) variable contingent upon the gender identity of their interlocutors – distinguishing between transgender and cisgender participants. This linguistic variation functions as a mechanism to counteract cis-normative gender ideologies and to manifest their nonbinary identities. Similar to how our participants vary their uptalk use depending on whether they are conversing with someone of the same gender or not, participants strategically adjust their (ING) use in accordance with the perceived security of different social spaces, employing this variation as a tool for identity positioning relative to other gender groups and to mitigate instances of being misgendered.

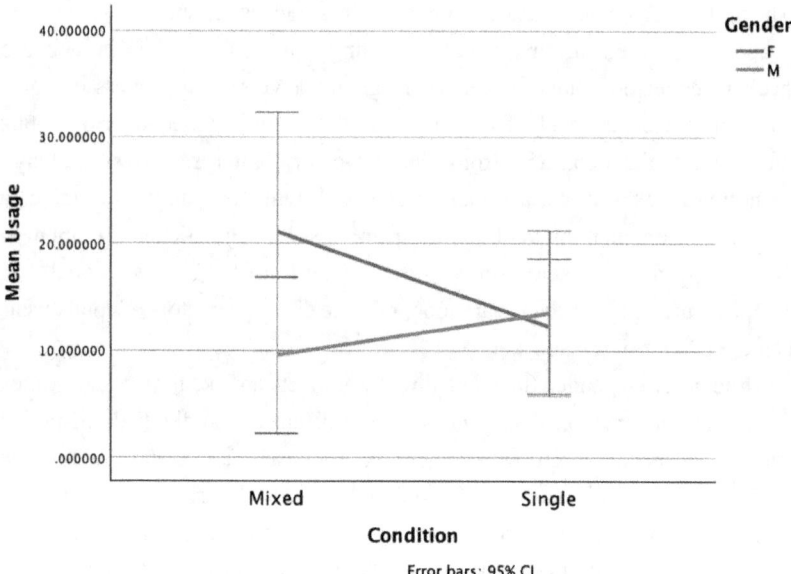

Figure 17 Mean uptalk usage (%) by gender and gender context.

Furthermore, it is worth noting that gender context and speaker gender interact ($pd = 0.99$). In single-gender settings, female and male speakers exhibit relatively similar uptalk usage rates, with male speakers (mean = 13.54%, SD = 9.27%) having slightly higher rates than women (mean = 12.23%, SD = 7.52%) overall. However, in mixed-sex contexts, uptalk usage rates are notably higher among women (mean = 21.16%, SD = 13.37%) and lower among men (mean = 9.59%, SD = 8.72%) (Figure 17). These results clearly indicate that gender context influences UPTALK, and the direction of this influence is modulated by the gender of the speaker. This is clear evidence of stylistic accommodation, as all speakers underwent both single and mixed-sex conditions.

But what exact mechanisms underlie the observed reduction in uptalk usage among men and its increase among women during cross-gender interactions? Our qualitative findings offer insights into this dynamic. Within same-gender groups, male listeners generally hold a favorable view of uptalk when employed by other males, while female listeners frequently assign negative indexical values to uptalk used by other females. This disparity could account for the higher incidence of uptalk among males compared to females. On the other hand, in mixed-gender interactions, where there may be an increased awareness of language use, the social meanings attributed to uptalk seem to invert. Male listeners, in the presence of a female speaker, are likely to perceive uptalk as indicative of a lack of education ("dumb," "not proficient"). When explicitly made aware of uptalk as a linguistic variable, these male listeners interpret it as signaling lack of proficiency, uncertainty, inauthenticity, femininity, and queerness, the latter two of which is considered of less value in a society that prizes hegemonic masculinity (e.g., "manly man") like Hong Kong. In contrast, in the context of a mixed-gender setup, female listeners often evaluate uptalk positively, associating it with higher education level, kindness, and being well traveled. And when uptalk is explicitly highlighted, although it is viewed by these female listeners as reflecting a lack of confidence, the use of uptalk is also seen as embodying femininity and emotionality – traits they consider positive. These findings elucidate how the gender of the audience could influence the social meanings of uptalk, explaining why men significantly reduce their use of uptalk and why women increase theirs in cross-gender conversations. This underscores the complexity of UPTALK's social meanings and cautions against oversimplifying the relationship between gender and uptalk, particularly in the context of Hong Kong.

Utterance Type

Our analysis, incorporating both descriptive and Bayesian modeling, indicates that the type of utterance – specifically, whether it is a hard fact, personal experience, explanation, or opinion – significantly influences UPTALK variation.

The categorization of utterance types is a modification of Levon's (2016) research, which coded the utterance types based on fact, opinion, explanation, description, and narrative. However, in practice, it occurred to us that the definitions of "description" and "narrative" may be convoluted, and it is difficult to differentiate the two. Therefore, we combined the categories into "personal experience," in which the speaker describes an event that they have experienced. Table 6 shows the definitions and examples of utterance types.

The utterances were first coded by three researchers separately. The results were then compared against each other, and all disagreements were resolved through discussion until the inter-rater agreement reached 100%.

We initially calculated uptalk proportions across different types of declarative statements, revealing distinct usage patterns: explanations (9.65%, $n = 96/995$), hard facts (14.16%, $n = 49/346$), opinions (12.17%, $n = 218/1,792$), and personal experiences (17.41%, $n = 215/1,235$). Subsequently, we incorporated utterance type into a regression model alongside other variables, confirming that utterance type remains a strong predictor of uptalk variation ($pd = 0.87$ to 1). This model showed that explanations are associated with the least uptalk, while personal experiences exhibit the most, as illustrated in Figure 18.

We posit that the observed pattern in which UPTALK is influenced by utterance type may be linked to stance-taking (Du Bois 2007; Gadanidis et al. 2023;

Table 6 Utterance type definitions and examples

Type	Definition	Example
Hard facts	Irrefutable statements	• *He comes from Indonesia.* • *His father and mother are also Chinese.*
Personal experience	Description of an event that the speaker has experienced	• *When I filled in the, uh, college form, uh, the top, my top priority is no FYP.* • *I have participated to ... NA, NA hall.*
Explanation	Elaboration on something previously stated, usually beginning with "I mean", "because".	• *I mean, I mean you ... after you graduate, you have a ... a thousand years to work.* • *Be, because her ... uh, Telegram name is Amy.*
Opinion	Personal beliefs and judgment	• *CUHK is very good.* • *But I think, ah, FYP is ... ah, laborious.*

Kiesling 2022), where the stances individuals adopt during specific utterances shape their employment of uptalk. Utilizing the "stance-taking" framework, we propose that uptalk is more prevalent in personal narratives, partially reflecting the speaker's affective stance, which pertains to the emotional position or attitude a speaker or writer holds toward the topic they are discussing, as can be seen in Gabriella's example.

(22) *It [uptalk] sounds like having some talk ... like having a speech to those secondary students. It's more like talking about his* **experience***. Much* **confident** *and very positive I would say.* (Gabriella)

Gabriella's observations suggest that uptalk functions as a discourse strategy within personal narratives, allowing speakers to express an affective stance that projects confidence and positivity while fostering listener engagement. This reinforces the idea that speakers strategically employ uptalk to sustain audience attention and encourage continued participation in the interaction. Tamara's personal account of her sleep habits during the production experiment provides an illustrative case for analyzing how uptalk operates to convey stance in personal narratives:

(23) *Like, I sometimes sleep to like, awake, be awake, for like, one* **hour** ↑ *And then ... three, three a.m. slept again ... I don't know* **why** ↑ (Tamara)

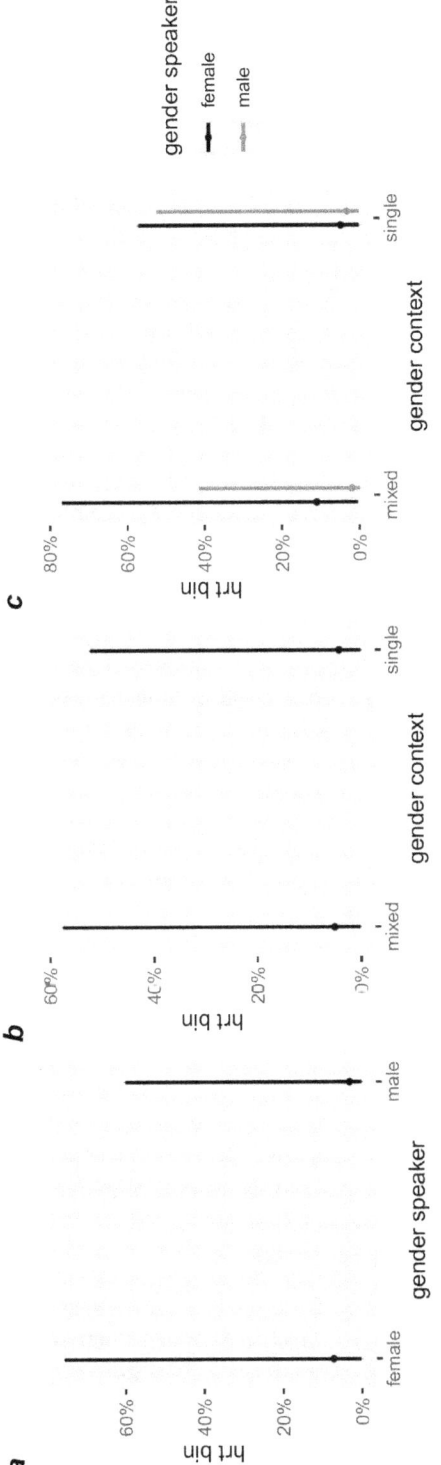

Figure 18 Marginal means: The effect of utterance type on UPTALK use.

In this excerpt, the rising intonation in "I don't know why ↑" externalizes uncertainty, indexing a hesitant stance, while simultaneously inviting affirmation (open-minded stance) from the listener. The prosodic contour reinforces both the speaker's open-mindedness and her emotional engagement with the narrative, inviting listener participation while maintaining speaker control through affective investment. Theodora's metalinguistic reflection explicitly articulates this interactive function of uptalk:

(24) *I think they are being careful. And maybe perhaps, when they use uptalk, it encourages people who are having conversation with them to sustain the conversation by maybe like guiding them to some answers because they, because they, as what you said, when people use uptalk, it sounds like a question. And it actually encourages the listeners to react or to give a response.* (Theodora)

Theodora's commentary highlights how uptalk fosters engagement by positioning the speaker as receptive to listener feedback, thus reinforcing the interactive nature of personal storytelling. This perspective aligns with broader discussions in sociolinguistics regarding the role of intonational features in facilitating dialogic exchange (Warren 2015; Lam 2020). Further evidence supporting the correlation between uptalk and personal narratives emerges in Theodora's reflection on her learning experiences and in Johnson's recounting of his stay at a friend's residence, both of which demonstrate "holding the floor" strategies:

(25) *Because I remember when I do some, like,* **research**↑ *And I was like, oh,* **okay**↑ (Theodora)

(26) *And they ... and ... we can ... when I stay at my friend's* **place**↑ *It's, like, very ... very* **annoying** ↑ (Johnson)

In these instances, the use of uptalk in "research↑" and "annoying↑" signals that the speaker has not yet completed their turn, thereby preempting interruptions and ensuring a fluid, uninterrupted narrative. Theodora's use of uptalk conveys a stance of surprise while simultaneously asserting conversational control, while Johnson's employment of uptalk indexes exasperation while maintaining his hold on the floor. These patterns reinforce the argument that uptalk is particularly prevalent in personal narratives due to its role in affective stance-taking, engagement strategies, and discourse management.

On the other hand, uptalk is least prevalent in explanatory contexts (and, as the results show, hard facts and opinions), possibly because such contexts often require an epistemic stance that reflects the speaker's certainty about the subject matter. When dealing with hard facts, opinions, and especially explanations, there is a notable reduction in uptalk usage, which may be attributed to its potential to diminish authority or assertiveness – a significant observation from our qualitative analysis. In more formal or informative settings, such as when providing opinions or explanations, speakers may avoid uptalk to preserve the authoritative or assertive quality of their statements. Explanatory speech typically necessitates a confident and certain tone to effectively communicate information or instructions. The use of a falling intonation at sentence ends, signaling completion and assertiveness, tends to be more fitting for contexts that demand an epistemic or authoritative stance.

Overall, the findings underscore that variables like utterance type and, consequently, stance-taking significantly influence uptalk usage, highlighting the critical role of socio-pragmatic context in understanding variations in uptalk.

5.3.4 Factors That Are Not Likely to Condition Uptalk

We incorporated certain factors into our model for which there was no substantive evidence to suggest a relationship with UPTALK. Specifically, variables such as ethnic identity, gender of the speaker, English proficiency, socioeconomic status or class, familiarity, institution, and awareness appear to have little direct influence on UPTALK. The lack of significant findings regarding the impact of ethnicity, class, and institutional affiliations on uptalk usage is consistent with our observations from the matched guise experiment and interview analysis. We noted that meanings such as "Chinese" and "Hong Konger" for ethnicity and "lower-class" or "upper-class" for socioeconomic status are not as salient as other meanings. Furthermore, institutional meanings of "CUHK" (The Chinese University of Hong Kong) and "HKU" (The University of Hong Kong) were not at all brought up during the interviews or experiment, indicating that uptalk does not generally and readily serve as a strong marker of ethnic, socioeconomic, or institutional identity.

The unexpected lack of evidence regarding the gender effect on uptalk usage, previously discussed, challenges the common sociolinguistic association of uptalk with femininity, particularly within the Hong Kong context where the connection is not as clear-cut. Other mediating factors may be influencing this relationship.

5.3.5 Relative Importance of Factors

An analysis of factors that have a high probability of influencing uptalk using the Boruta algorithm reveals that not all factors hold equal weight in predicting or analyzing uptalk variation (see supplementary resources). This analysis, which focuses on noninteraction factors and those previously identified as highly probable factors for conditioning uptalk use, demonstrates that individual stylistic factors or individual-level characteristics and the dynamics within speaker interactions (i.e., conversation pair) are the most dominant influences, relative to other factors. The most critical determinant, based on the algorithmic random-forests-based analysis, is the individual characteristics of the participants, with a mean importance score of 20.60 (Rank 1), suggesting that uptalk is profoundly influenced by preferences that relate to the individual. Similarly, the dynamics within conversational pairs, with a mean importance of 15.83 (Rank 2), underscore how relational aspects, the topics discussed, and interaction patterns shape uptalk usage.

However, other factors such as the type of utterance, the broader gender context alone, age, and the sentiment of the utterance show relatively lower impacts, with importance scores ranging from 8.81 to 2.50. These factors, while highly probable in conditioning uptalk, are significantly less influential in conditioning the variable, highlighting the unequal levels of importance among the factors. The discussed importance asymmetry underscores the complexity of uptalk as a sociolinguistic phenomenon, emphasizing that while some factors are critical for understanding uptalk variation in the context of HKE, others contribute less significantly.

5.3.6 The Interactions of Factors with Gender

Earlier, we hypothesized that in Hong Kong, gender will interact with other social or "extralinguistic" factors to condition UPTALK based on prior studies that have identified complex interactions between gender and other factors (Labov 1984; Guy et al. 1986; Eckert 1989). We expected UPTALK would carry distinct, context-dependent gendered meanings within various social groups or networks in Hong Kong. This was the case in our qualitative data, where we found some evidence of interactions between gender and other factors. For example, we found class-related meanings of the use of uptalk varied depending on the gender of the speaker. For instance, Tyler viewed uptalk in men as indicative of education, yet saw it as a sign of unintelligence in women. Similarly, while Tamara did not attribute ethnic meanings of "Hong Kong-ness" to uptalk used by men, she observed such associations in women's usage. Gia considered uptalk in men to suggest youthfulness, a perception not extended to women. The evidence suggests that the social meanings of uptalk, encompassing meanings related to ethnicity, education, and age, may be influenced by or interact with the gender of the speaker. However, it is uncertain whether this relationship is reciprocal: Do the gendered meanings (e.g., femininity) of uptalk shift according to the social group or other factors? Specifically, does the impact of gender on uptalk apply universally, or is it shaped by other social factors?

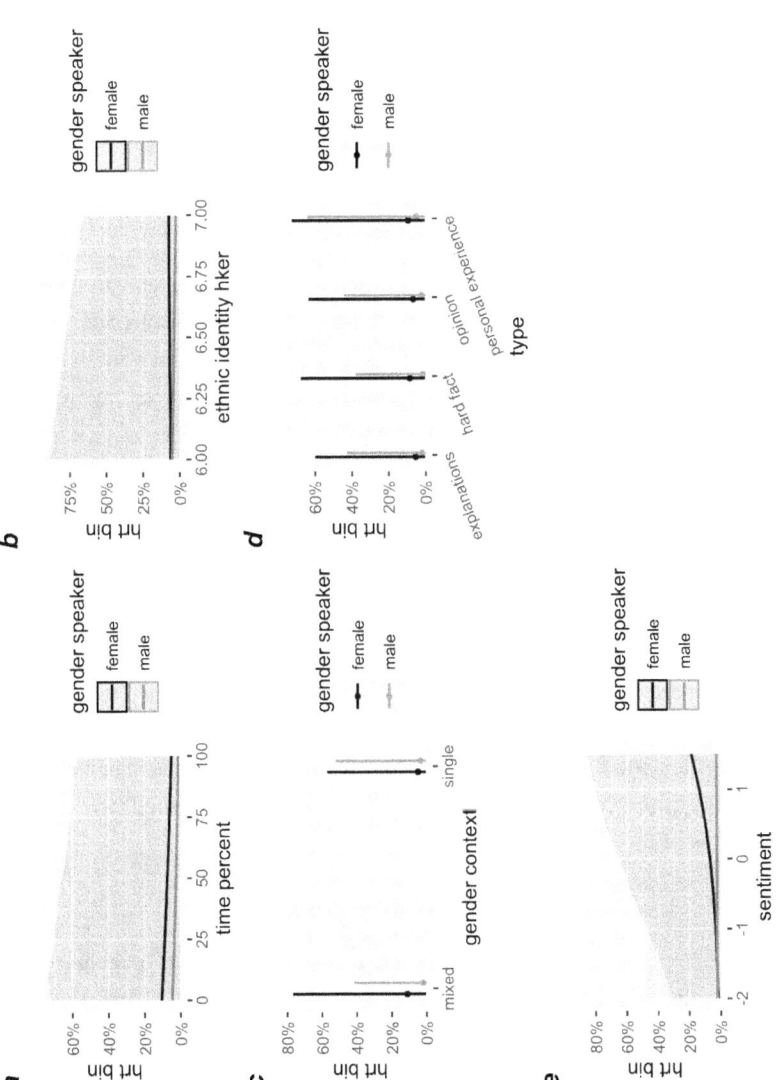

Figure 19 Marginal means: Interactions between gender and selected factors on conditioning UPTALK use.

Our quantitative findings suggest that the gendered meanings (e.g., femininity) of UPTALK may indeed vary by social group or other factors (Figure 19). This is indicated by different rates of uptalk usage among men and women, which we interpret as potential gendered meanings in the use of uptalk (e.g., associating uptalk with femininity) that differ across specific social groups or conditions. Although there are factors that we currently do not have evidence of mediating the effect of gender on uptalk use such as ethnicity (Chinese), English proficiency, age, socioeconomic status of class, familiarity, institution, and awareness, we do find other factors that modulate the relationship between gender and uptalk, which we detail next.

Time and Gender

One notable discovery is the interaction between time and gender: Overall, women's use of uptalk decreased more rapidly over the session compared to men's. Initially, women employed uptalk significantly more than men, but by the end of the session, the frequency of uptalk usage between men and women had nearly equalized. It is unclear why exactly the women in our study exhibited this pattern, but one possible factor may be because of a broader sociolinguistic phenomenon where women, sensitive and aware of the stereotypical associations of uptalk with uncertainty and submissiveness (see qualitative results), implicitly or explicitly reduce its use to assert more authority and confidence as conversations progress. This adaptation could reflect a strategic shift in register or style, aligning their speech patterns more closely with those of their hegemonic male counterparts, who are stereotypically believed to use less uptalk, based on the qualitative results. In addition, the observed decrease of uptalk use among women could also be influenced by the dynamics of the specific interaction, such as the topic of discussion, the formality of the setting, and the roles or identities of the speakers involved.

Ethnicity and Gender

Another finding was that gender influences UPTALK differently depending on ethnic identity, particularly Hong Konger identity. Our analysis indicates that among individuals less identified with Hong Konger identity, uptalk usage is similar across genders. However, for those more strongly identified as Hong Konger, a significant disparity emerges: Women exhibit a higher usage of uptalk compared to men, who use it minimally. This pattern suggests that uptalk may convey a joint meaning of "feminine" and "Hong Konger." Although tempting, it is premature to associate this usage directly with the stereotypical "Kong Girl" persona, as no direct links have been established in the data.

The quantitative results demonstrating that gender and ethnicity jointly influence uptalk usage align only partially with qualitative insights. Specific speakers, such as Emery and Tamara, associate uptalk in women's speech with Hong Konger identity, whereas this association diminishes when they evaluate men's speech. In contrast, other participants, namely Samuel and Johnson, attribute uptalk predominantly to Hong Konger identity in men's speech, not observing this pattern in women. This divergence between quantitative production patterns and qualitative perception findings highlights a disparity: Increased uptalk among Hong Konger women (i.e., social variation) does not uniformly correspond with societal perceptions or evaluations across both genders (i.e., the "Hong Konger" interpretation in both men and women's use of uptalk by listeners). Perhaps other factors, such as other mediating factors, are at play here that led to such a divergent finding.

Overall, the findings reveal two key points: First, the relationship between social variation and explicit social meanings or evaluations, such as stereotypes, is not necessarily straightforward, particularly in the context of Hong Kong. Second, the data confirm that on the production level, gender and ethnicity interact to influence uptalk variation.

Utterance Type and Gender

The interaction between utterance type and gender in UPTALK emerges distinctly within the context of our study. Female participants exhibited a marked increase in uptalk during the articulation of declaratives conveying unequivocal hard facts, as opposed to their delivery of explanations, opinions, or personal anecdotes. In these latter contexts, the disparity in uptalk frequency between genders diminished notably. Conversely, male participants demonstrated a reduced propensity for uptalk across explanations and subjective utterances such as opinions, and an even further reduction in its usage within factual declarations.

Determining the precise reasons for these gendered patterns in uptalk remains challenging; however, insights from the collected qualitative data shed light on potential motivations. Our qualitative analysis indicates that female participants often interpret uptalk as a marker of uncertainty and a reflection of diminished confidence. Male participants, in contrast, predominantly associate uptalk with femininity, while also linking it to a range of other social markers, including expressiveness, humor, identification with the LGBTQ community, and lower proficiency in English. These associations were less pronounced or altogether absent in the responses female participants provided.

We suspect that the varying explicit interpretations of uptalk between genders, rather than the gender differences per se, significantly influence uptalk patterns within specific socio-pragmatic contexts, such as when expressing opinions or stating hard facts. Women, possibly aiming to preserve interpersonal harmony or avoid confrontation, tend to employ more uptalk when presenting hard facts. In their view, uptalk signals uncertainty and lack of confidence – traits they consider positive as these may soften the assertiveness of factual statements, thereby aligning with notions of politeness as proposed by Brown and Levinson's (1987) politeness theory. On the other hand, men display a distinct pattern, utilizing minimal uptalk in factual statements as compared to opinions or more subjective expressions. Our qualitative data suggest that men associate uptalk with humor, LGBTQ identities, and lower English proficiency – attributes that are not typically advantageous or appropriate in contexts that demand high levels of certainty and objectivity, such as factual declarations. Thus men who perceive uptalk through such lenses (like the male participants in our study) are likely to use it sparingly, particularly when the situation calls for conveying confidence and precision, traits highly valued in epistemically strong or objective statements.

Overall, the analysis reveals that the impact of gender on uptalk is not uniform or universally applicable, but is instead mediated by socio-pragmatic variables such as the nature of the utterance. The qualitative data further illuminate this observation, suggesting that the differential use of uptalk among men and women across various declarative contexts is likely attributable to the disparate significations attached to uptalk by each gender. These findings underscore the complexity of gender as a variable in sociolinguistic research, particularly in its interaction with pragmatic elements of communication.

5.3.7 The Role of Awareness

Earlier in this Element, we established that awareness influences the social meanings attributed to UPTALK. Individuals who are aware of uptalk often interpret it differently compared to when they are unaware of this speech pattern. In this section, we delve deeper into how awareness affects uptalk by exploring its interactions with all previously discussed factors, which are integrated into our Bayesian model. While our qualitative analysis has concentrated on how awareness conditions the social meanings of UPTALK, here, our aim is to examine how awareness modulates the relationship between the actual use of uptalk and the factors in our model. Additionally, we seek to confirm and possibly expand upon our qualitative findings.

Prior to delving deeper into our analysis, it is essential to articulate the operational definition of "awareness" employed in this study. "Awareness" is quantified specifically through the frequency with which participants overestimate their employment of uptalk. This operationalization is based on the discrepancies observed between participants' perceived and actual use of uptalk, under the assumption that individuals who neither underestimate nor overestimate their use when queried about their frequency of uptalk demonstrate a heightened level of "awareness." It is important to note that the "awareness" variable in this context is confined to a general, individual-level awareness and does not extend to cognitive or contextual awareness at the event level. Accordingly, we advocate for a cautious interpretation of our findings, acknowledging the limited scope of "awareness" as defined in our study.

Our analysis of the interplay between awareness and the variables included in our model reveals that seven factors demonstrate interactions with awareness (Figure 20): time, ethnicity (specifically Chinese), English proficiency, speaker's gender, gender context, type of utterance, and sentiment. For the remaining variables, our findings do not provide sufficient evidence to confirm an interaction. In what follows, we discuss notable findings on the role of awareness in mediating the relationship between these factors and uptalk use.

Proficiency and Awareness

We discovered that awareness significantly modulates the relationship between English proficiency and the usage of uptalk. Among participants with a heightened awareness of their uptalk usage, those who rated themselves as highly proficient English users were observed to suppress their use of uptalk, whereas their less proficient counterparts exhibited an increased usage. In contrast, among those with lower awareness levels, a divergent pattern emerged: Individuals with high English proficiency tended to increase their uptalk usage, while those with lower proficiency tended to reduce it.

Our qualitative findings suggest that the observed trend in proficiency and the impact of awareness can be explained by differing social evaluations of UPTALK based on awareness levels. To recapitulate, those who had low awareness of uptalk perceived it as indicative of "high proficiency in English," "educated," and "okay English." In contrast, those highly aware of uptalk predominantly viewed it as a sign of "less proficiency" and "less education," and by extension, less "standard." The explicit perceptions might explain why, in the production task, self-reported proficient English speakers who are aware of their uptalk usage often minimize the use of uptalk. These speakers, recognizing the "less proficiency" and "nonstandard" meanings of uptalk, reduce uptalk to appear (even) more proficient. The findings of the qualitative explicit evaluations could also explain why individuals who are highly aware of uptalk use and those who consider themselves less proficient in English seem to be using more uptalk. In

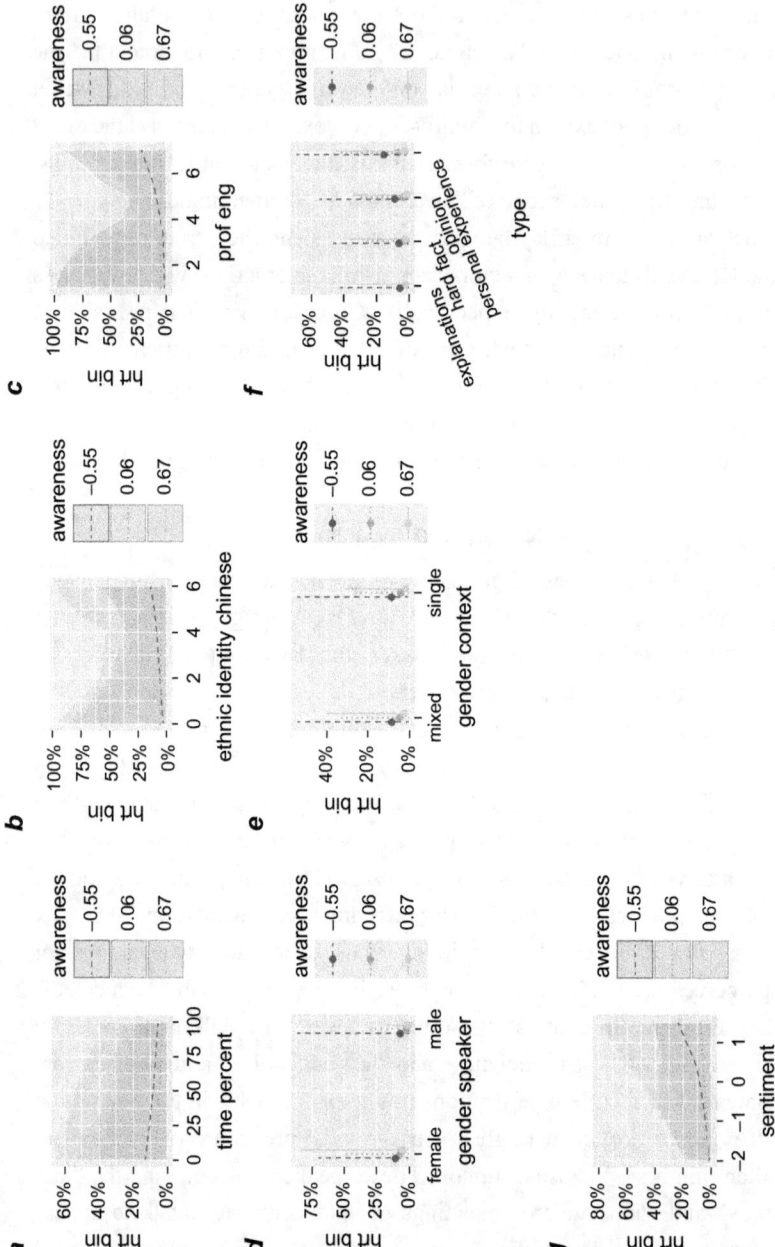

Figure 20 Marginal means: Interactions between awareness and selected factors on conditioning UPTALK use.

their case, the increased use of uptalk indexes their cautious stance and presents to listeners their English limitations, a warranted account given that uptalk is often associated with "uncertainty" in Hong Kong.

The differing behavior among those *less* aware of uptalk usage, where less proficient English speakers use limited uptalk and more proficient speakers use it extensively, might be explained by the implicit interpretations of uptalk. Our qualitative data suggest that the "nonstandard" connotations of uptalk are prominent only among those who are explicitly aware of its use. In instances where there is less explicit awareness, uptalk is sometimes even seen as an indicator of high English proficiency. We suspect that individuals who are less explicitly aware of their uptalk use and report high proficiency in English exhibit increased rates of uptalk due to a lack of incentive to curb its use; in fact, they may be motivated to use uptalk as it signals greater English proficiency in this context. In contrast, individuals who report lower proficiency may use uptalk less frequently, attempting to avoid seeming overly proficient and risking loss of face. This is again possible because of the implicit indexical association of uptalk with higher English proficiency.

Gender and Awareness

In alignment with the overarching theme of this Element, we conclude our discussion by exploring how awareness modulates the interplay between gender and uptalk utilization. This study has shown that an individual's explicit awareness of UPTALK significantly conditions the manifestation of gender differences in its use. Our analyses indicate that, among those participants less aware of their uptalk usage, there is a relative parity between men and women in the frequency of uptalk, with men exhibiting marginally higher rates and greater variability. Notably, certain male participants displayed uptalk rates significantly surpassing those of female counterparts. In stark contrast, among those more cognizant of their uptalk, a significant divergence emerges: Male participants demonstrate a markedly reduced usage of uptalk, whereas female participants significantly increase their use, compared to their less aware female peers. Additionally, our findings revealed a gradation in awareness: Individuals with moderate awareness of their uptalk usage exhibit patterns akin to those with high awareness, yet distinctly different from those with minimal awareness.

The modulating effect of awareness on the gender–UPTALK link becomes further evident when considering the context or composition of gender in uptalk usage. Our analysis reveals that among participants with lower levels of explicit awareness, uptalk usage does not significantly differ between those in single-gender groups and those in mixed-gender groups. In contrast, participants who are highly aware of their uptalk use demonstrate a pronounced increase in uptalk rates during mixed-gender interactions compared to their less aware counterparts. These findings underscore that the gender composition of conversational contexts gains salience in shaping uptalk dynamics particularly when participants are highly aware of their linguistic behavior. This heightened awareness appears to be a prerequisite for the strategic or stylistic use of uptalk as a means of constructing gender identities in social interactions at least in the case of HKE.

However, it remains to be questioned whether mixed-gender groups consistently exhibit higher uptalk rates than single-gender groups when participants are highly aware of their language use, and whether the gender of the speaker significantly conditions the interplay between gender composition and uptalk usage. The data resoundingly refute this assumption. In-depth analysis reveals that among those least aware of their uptalk, the speaker's gender does not strongly affect the relationship between gender composition and uptalk usage. The patterns of uptalk remain consistent across different gender compositions, with a marginally higher incidence of uptalk among men engaging with other men. Yet, as awareness heightens, the influence of gender becomes pronounced: Women's uptalk usage significantly exceeds that of men. Additionally, transitioning from single-gender to mixed-gender contexts, there is a notable increase in uptalk usage (Figure 21). In contrast, men's uptalk usage markedly decreases, becoming minimal or nearly absent in mixed-gender settings compared to single-gender contexts.

The results compellingly demonstrate that the gender of the speaker significantly influences the modulating effect of awareness on the relationship between gender composition and uptalk usage. Furthermore, they underscore that patterns of linguistic accommodation are predominantly conscious endeavors. Specifically, when speakers are aware of their uptalk use, the production patterns align with their evaluative perceptions – where uptalk is associated by men with attributes typically regarded as "feminine," such as

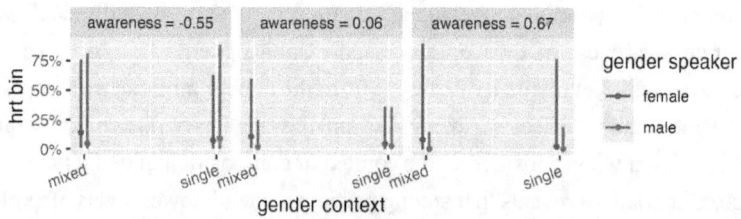

Figure 21 Marginal means: Interactions between awareness, gender context, and gender of speaker. Legend: female (left), male (lighter shade, right).

being emotional, or linked to LGBTQ identities. In contrast, when speakers are unaware of their uptalk, it is not strongly coded with either queer/gay or feminine connotations. This observation aligns with earlier qualitative assessments, indicating that men, when explicitly managing their uptalk, tend to minimize its use due to its association with femininity and queer identities – attributes not traditionally esteemed within the Hong Kong constructs of hegemonic masculinity that prize a "manly man" persona (Liong 2010).

This account gains further credence by observing the gradual shifts in uptalk patterns from low to high awareness. For instance, men with moderate awareness of uptalk still employ it in mixed-gender settings, albeit not as minimally as those with high awareness, nor as frequently as those with low awareness. This gradation lends substantial weight to the interpretation that men and women, influenced by prominent gendered meanings of uptalk, exhibit divergent usage patterns. Such behavior appears to align with and accommodate hegemonic societal expectations, wherein men are anticipated to avoid "feminine" speech patterns, and women are expected to conform to "feminine" norms through their uptalk usage.

Overall, the findings offer robust evidence that awareness significantly modulates the impact of gender on uptalk production patterns. This modulation is likely tied to the gendered meanings that are activated when speakers become explicitly aware of their uptalk use. Additionally, the local Hong Kong context, which valorizes hegemonic masculinity and marginalizes uptalk that codes the speaker as "feminine," plays a crucial role in shaping these patterns.

5.3.8 Summary

In Table 7, we summarize the insights garnered from our quantitative investigation into the various conditioning factors of UPTALK.

We find that temporal, stylistic, and social factors such as the timing, participant involvement, and dynamics within conversation pairs are good predictors of uptalk use. Socio-pragmatic factors like the type of utterance also significantly impact uptalk, particularly in how they interact with gender. Additionally, affective factors – that is, sentiment – prominently affect uptalk and exhibit a notable interaction with both gender and awareness.

Our analysis has also identified factors that are not likely to condition uptalk, as indicated by the gray cells in the table. These include proficiency in English, age, socioeconomic status or class, familiarity, and ethnic identity specific to Hong Kongers, which show either a neutral influence or are less significant in their impact compared to other factors. This differentiation in the results points to the nuanced ways in which uptalk functions across different contexts and

Table 7 Summary of quantitative results (+++ 0.9–1, ++ 0.8–0.9, + 0.7–0.8, ~ 0.6–0.7)

Type	Factor	Conditions HRT?	Relative importance (without interactions) (Boruta)	Interaction with gender of speaker?	Effect moderated by awareness?
Temporal	Time	+++	average	++	~
Social	Conversation Pair	+++	higher	NA	NA
	Proficiency (English)				+
	Gender of speaker			NA	~
	Gender context	+	lower	+++	++
	Gender context x Gender of speaker	+++	higher	NA	NA, but yes, descriptively
	Age	~	lower		
	Socioeconomic status or class				
	Familiarity				
	Institution				
Socio-pragmatic	Utterance type (Stance)	+++	average	+++	+++
Cognitive	Awareness			~	NA

demographics, illustrating that while many factors contribute to the use of uptalk, their effects vary in importance and are intertwined with the speaker's gender and awareness in various degrees.

6 Comparison of Quantitative and Qualitative Data

In this section, we align the principal outcomes of UPTALK production and evaluation within Table 8, concentrating exclusively on variables analyzed for their relation to speaker awareness to ensure comparability. Our analysis of the selected eleven factors reveals that three exhibit discrepancies between production and evaluation (e.g., age, socioeconomic class, ethnic identity), four show partial alignment (e.g., gender context, institution), and four align completely (e.g., English proficiency, gender of speaker). This comparison indicates that the relationship between uptalk production and evaluation is not uniformly consistent; rather, it varies, sometimes contrasting starkly.

Through our comparative analysis, we draw several pertinent conclusions: First, it is evident that speakers explicitly employ uptalk to signify non-Chinese identity, diminished English proficiency, and femininity. This is substantiated through the observation of production patterns aligning with participant evaluations, such as the observation that individuals with high

Table 8 Comparison of production and evaluation data (N.E. = no evidence, + = increased, – = decreased)

Factor	Production		Evaluation		Production-Perception Match?
	less aware	more aware	less aware	more aware	
Ethnic identity (+ non-Chinese)	– uptalk	+ uptalk	N.E.	present	match
Ethnic identity (+ Hong Konger)	N.E.	N.E.	present	N.E.	partial
Proficiency in English (higher)	+ uptalk	– uptalk	present	N.E.	match
Gender of speaker (women/feminine)	– uptalk	+ uptalk	present	dominant	match
Gender context (mixed)	– uptalk	+ uptalk	N.E.	N.E.	partial
Gender context x Gender of speaker (women in mixed-gender context)	– uptalk	+ uptalk	N.E.	N.E.	partial
Age (younger)	– uptalk	– uptalk	present	present	mismatch
Socioeconomic status or class (lower/middle class)	N.E.	N.E.	present	present	mismatch
Familiarity (high)	N.E.	N.E.	present	present	mismatch
Institution	N.E.	N.E.	N.E.	N.E.	match

English proficiency avoid uptalk, a feature that was explicitly noted to be indicative of lower English proficiency. Additionally, uptalk's association with femininity is corroborated by its prevalent use among women. These attributes – femininity, limited English proficiency, and non-Chinese identity – can be regarded as stereotypically linked to uptalk, embodying characteristics that are broadly recognized, tied to specific social groups (e.g., women), and frequently discussed, as reflected in our interview and evaluative data (Labov 1972b).

Second, our analysis identifies certain meanings associated with uptalk that, while not currently mirroring social variation in production data, hold potential for future stylistic utilization. We delineate four broad sociolinguistic patterns of uptalk that emerge from our study (see supplementary resources for detailed table), grounded in differing levels of speaker awareness, social evaluation, and usage contexts. These patterns reveal varying degrees of mismatches between production and evaluation, suggesting that while some may not currently serve stylistic functions, they could potentially be adapted for such purposes in the future.

The first pattern involves latent stereotypical relationships (i.e., "latent stereotype"), such as those involving Hong Konger identity, where uptalk is implicitly associated with these meanings, yet the social meanings do not correspond with relevant patterns of uptalk sociolinguistic variations. The second pattern represents a claimed or reported stereotype, where uptalk is judged and claimed to carry certain meanings – such as youth, lower class, and high familiarity – irrespective of speaker awareness, though these do not align with observable and relevant patterns of sociolinguistic variation. The third involves cases where uptalk functions as an "indicator" of certain social meanings (Labov 1972b), for example, mixed gender, feminine in mixed-gender settings. Here, uptalk is not evaluated with these meanings, but speakers of relevant social groups or speakers placed in relevant contexts use it profusely. Last, the fourth pattern identifies uptalk as a "marker" of positivity (Labov 1972b), where its use is confined predominantly to speakers in positive contexts and by those less aware of its sociolinguistic implications.

Third, we confidently identified factors that are not indexically linked to uptalk, specifically institutional affiliation. The lack of social variation and commentary on uptalk related to institutions, such as CUHK versus HKU, suggests it is improbable that uptalk will acquire meanings associated with specific educational institutions or be used stylistically to signify membership within them, at least based on the current data.

7 General Discussion

This section further integrates the findings recently discussed and addressed the three primary hypotheses introduced at the beginning of this Element, and, when possible, links our findings to the broader literature on gender and language.

7.1 Hypothesis 1: Uptalk, Femininity, and Other Social Meanings

The initial hypothesis we proposed suggested that the use of uptalk would primarily convey connotations or meanings that could be ideologically linked and interpreted as "feminine." Additionally, we anticipated that uptalk would have other meanings not directly associated with gender, such as informality. Our quantitative and qualitative data confirm this hypothesis, consistent with Britain's (1992) findings for New Zealand English.

Adopting a contemporary, multilayered approach to understanding the connections between meaning and language, one potential explanation for uptalk's association with feminine social meanings (e.g., "feminine," "woman," "female") is its indexing of uncertainty, emotionality, and cooperative communication. These qualities are ideologically linked to "stereotypical" feminine traits. For example, Levon (2016) suggested that women use uptalk as both an instrumental and affective tool to uphold epistemic authority while minimizing perceived threats to the listener. This view aligns particularly with our qualitative findings, where several participants noted that women employ uptalk as an affiliative tactic to encourage agreement or further the conversation. This indicates that participants might leverage the cooperative aspects of uptalk (i.e., its indexical meanings) and relate them to "stereotypical" feminine personae. This connection likely accounts for uptalk's strong association with feminine social meanings and also explains why it is linked with other meanings such as uncertainty, lack of confidence, tentativeness, and emotionality. These associations are consistent with various studies on uptalk or HRT, which have identified connections between uptalk and uncertainty.

However, we have discovered that gendered meanings are not consistently triggered. An important nuance revealed by our study is that gendered meanings, especially "feminine" ones, become more pronounced only when speakers are more aware of uptalk as a linguistic feature. While it is unclear if this pattern holds in other contexts where uptalk is prevalent, in the context of Hong Kong and HKE, the gendered connotations of uptalk become more apparent with heightened awareness. This insight enhances our understanding of uptalk as a sociolinguistic variable in Hong Kong.

We have also learned that the gendered interpretations of UPTALK are not isolated phenomena. These interpretations are deeply interconnected with broader social meanings, a linkage evident in the qualitative data where participants attributed uptalk not solely to gender, but also to other social categories during discussions. The quantitative production data further elucidates the influence of nongender factors on uptalk variation, demonstrating the complex interplay between gender and other sociolinguistic factors. These results decisively confirm that uptalk carries additional meanings that extend beyond gendered interpretations, reinforcing theories from the bottom-up perspective on gender. This perspective posits that societal perceptions of gender are composed of intersectional identities (e.g., young, female Hong Konger or Kong Girl persona), which are inherently gendered to varying degrees.

In addition to gendered interpretations, our study demonstrates that in HKE, uptalk functions as a highly affiliative communicative tool, facilitating affective interactions and enhancing solidarity among interlocutors. This stands in contrast to the conclusions drawn by Cheng and Warren (2005), who argued that uptalk in Hong Kong indexes assertion and dominance. Our qualitative analysis presents a more nuanced view, identifying two distinct uses of uptalk. The first involves employing uptalk to convey a gentler, less aggressive tone.

Although uptalk may reflect tentativeness, it concurrently signals openness and a readiness to reach consensus in discourse. This aligns with prior research suggesting that uptalk can soften the potential for disagreement and strengthen speaker-hearer solidarity (Britain 1992). The second usage involves employing uptalk to imbue speech with emotional depth and engagement. Our qualitative findings indicate that several participants recognized the affective and engaging functions of uptalk, noting that a rise in pitch in declarative sentences introduces tonal variation, rendering the speech less monotone. This enhances the narrative's engagement, helping the speaker appear less mechanical and more emotionally expressive.

We propose that the affiliative function of uptalk may vary depending on the familiarity of the listeners. It is plausible that when addressing familiar listeners, the primary objective of employing uptalk is to create an engaging tone that fosters conversational exchange. In contrast, the use of uptalk with unfamiliar listeners may primarily aim to project a less aggressive demeanor. Future studies could explore the mediating influence of listener familiarity on the affiliative social meanings associated with uptalk.

7.2 Hypothesis 2: Gender and UPTALK Production

Our second hypothesis conjectures a correlation between gender and HKE speakers' use of UPTALK. We hypothesized that women, engaging actively with the "feminine" meanings (among other meanings) observed in the evaluation task, would exhibit a higher frequency of uptalk usage compared to their male counterparts. However, the evidence, as discussed in Section 6, presents a nuanced picture that does not entirely substantiate this hypothesis. We found that temporal dynamics, gender contexts, ethnic identities, utterance types, and sentiment have demonstrable interactions with gender in shaping uptalk variations. However, we lack sufficient evidence to assert similar interactions for factors such as Chinese ethnic identity, English proficiency, age, socioeconomic class, familiarity, or institutional affiliations. This necessitates further analytic endeavors to confirm these interactions and to quantify their impacts on uptalk usage. Importantly, a deeper investigation through qualitative methodologies and detailed interviews is imperative. By examining individual engagements with uptalk (e.g., through the performance of personae), one can achieve a nuanced understanding of how gender interacts with various factors to influence uptalk usage. Such detailed insights will illuminate the specific contexts in which gendered meanings are invoked and the particular gendered scenarios that activate certain social meanings of uptalk.

7.3 Hypothesis 3: The Role of Awareness

Our third research question examines the extent to which patterns in UPTALK evaluation diverge from those observed in its production, specifically investigating the role of explicit and implicit awareness. Correspondingly, our third hypothesis posits that in contexts where speakers exhibit heightened awareness of UPTALK, at least some speakers of HKE who use uptalk will explicitly associate it with femininity. Furthermore, we hypothesize that UPTALK will be mobilized differently across gendered contexts, such as same-gender versus mixed-gender interactions.

Although uptalk is widely perceived as a linguistic feature associated with femininity, our production data indicate that women do not categorically use uptalk more frequently than men. This finding challenges a straightforward alignment between uptalk production and its social evaluation. However, when incorporating speaker awareness into the analysis, our results reveal support for the hypothesis: In contexts where explicit awareness of uptalk is heightened, women exhibit increased uptalk production, which aligns with heightened associations of uptalk with femininity. In contrast, in contexts where awareness is lower, uptalk production is reduced, and explicit associations with femininity diminish. This pattern extends beyond gender to other social variables, including ethnic identity (Chinese), English proficiency, and institutional affiliation. In contrast, notable disparities emerge in the relationship between uptalk production and evaluation across awareness contexts, particularly with respect to age, socioeconomic status, and familiarity. Additionally, only partial congruence is observed in gendered interactional contexts and within ethnic identity categories (Hong Konger).

In instances where mismatches between production and evaluation emerge, our findings suggest that uptalk's associations with social meanings are not uniform. Instead, they function in heterogeneous ways, manifesting as "latent stereotypes," "claimed stereotypes," "indicators," or "markers" of specific meanings, such as positivity (see discussion in Section 6). Our comparative analysis of production and evaluation data underscores that the relationship between uptalk production and evaluation is not consistently aligned; rather, it exhibits significant variability, sometimes revealing stark contrasts. This highlights the complexity of the indexical field surrounding uptalk and cautions against simplistically equating production patterns with evaluation trends in sociolinguistic research.

On the varied *explicit* mobilization of uptalk across gendered contexts such as same-gender versus mixed-gender interactions, we find that men tend to reduce their use of uptalk, whereas women increase it, particularly in cross-gender interactions. This suggests that uptalk production is not merely a reflexive linguistic feature but rather an indexically rich resource mediated by social expectations. Specifically, men's minimization of uptalk may reflect an alignment with hegemonic masculinity norms that privilege assertiveness, while women's increased usage appears to be consistent with affiliative and politeness-driven interactional strategies. These findings lend further support to the argument that uptalk is explicitly associated with femininity, reinforcing the broader claim that its social meaning is contextually contingent and strategically mobilized within gendered interactions.

Regarding the impact of gendered contexts, such as mixed-gender versus single-gender settings, our findings diverge significantly from previous Western research. Levon (2016) found that men in Western contexts use uptalk more frequently in mixed-gender interactions, whereas Leaper and Ayres's (2007) meta-analysis suggested that gender differences in assertive and affiliative speech are more pronounced in same-sex groups. In contrast, our data indicate that men in Hong Kong use uptalk slightly less in mixed-gender settings than in single-gender contexts, suggesting that gendered interpretations of uptalk are variable. Additionally, our findings show a higher overall tendency for uptalk use in mixed-gender conversations compared to same-gender interactions. Notably, women's uptalk usage is significantly higher in mixed-gender settings, suggesting a form of gender-based speech accommodation. Our data suggest that women may feel an increased need to be affiliative and polite when speaking with men. This aligns with previous research, such as that of Britain (1992) and Kiesling (2005), who propose that uptalk can be mobilized stylistically to convey femininity, politeness, and informality. This finding contradicts Leaper and Ayres's (2007) meta-analysis, which found stronger sociolinguistic differentiation in same-gender settings.

Several factors could explain the disparities between findings in Asian and Western contexts. First, the differences could stem from regional differences in how prosodic features are employed by Westerners and Hong Kong participants. Second, the proficiency and familiarity with English among our Hong Kong participants, for whom English is a second language, might impact their use of uptalk. This contrasts with Western participants in previous studies, who generally used their "native" language, thereby possibly accounting for the observed discrepancies. Third, adopting a social constructionist perspective, divergent conceptions of masculinity and femininity in Asia and the West may also contribute to the observed variation in UPTALK. They could influence participants' motivations to construct and express gendered personae in interactions with the same or different gender. This effect may be particularly pronounced in Hong Kong, where gendered personae such as the "Kong Girl" (feminine) are often juxtaposed with masculine archetypes like the "Hong Kong father" or "new good men" on axes of affiliativeness and assertiveness, the latter of which is related to demonstrations of hegemonic masculinity, including exerting "control" (Liong 2010: 331). We believe that this could at least partially explain the gendered sociolinguistic patterns described by Carli (1990), wherein the gender effect on language use becomes particularly salient in mixed-gender settings relative to single-gender settings. According to Carli's (1990) proposition, in mixed-gender contexts, men are likely to dominate the conversation and employ more assertive speech patterns (i.e., less uptalk), while women may exhibit more submissive behavior and use more affiliative speech (i.e., more uptalk), which is consistent with our observations. Compared to the West, where such patterns are less apparent (e.g., in New Zealand courtrooms) (Innes 2007), our findings suggest that the concept of "femininity" in Hong Kong differs from that in other contexts, thereby influencing the sociolinguistic patterning associated with uptalk.

8 Conclusion

This Element endeavors to explore the potential impacts of gender on the prosodic stylistic variation of UPTALK within "mainstream" HKE. While the principal focus remains on the role of gender, our comprehensive literature review has illuminated the intersection of gender with other sociodemographic variables such as age, class, ethnicity, and affective states. Accordingly, this research aims to explore the extent to which these factors influence uptalk usage in Hong Kong and their possible interactions with gender. Specifically, we investigate whether factors like explicit sociolinguistic awareness (Dodsworth 2005) mediate or moderate gender's influence on UPTALK, drawing inspiration from Levon (2016). The ultimate goal is to delineate the social meanings that uptalk conveys within the Hong Kong context. Through the deployment of diverse methodologies applied to a cohort of sixteen participants from Hong Kong, we have refined our understanding of UPTALK's usage and social perception. The insights gained from this comprehensive investigation are encapsulated in the following key takeaways, detailed subsequently.

1. ***Complexity of uptalk meanings.*** UPTALK is linked to multiple social meanings (e.g., lack of confidence, uncertainty, emotionality, low education), and these meanings can be, but are not always, ideologically linked to gender. Gendered meanings intersect and interact with other meanings (e.g., sexuality, geography, ethnicity, age, class) in complex ways, such as through

gendered identities and personae (e.g., "nerd school girl," "Kong girl," "Hong Kong father").

2. **Gender-dependent meanings and gendered accommodation.** Although not the most salient factor, both production and evaluation of UPTALK are influenced by the gender of both interlocutors (e.g., listener, speaker), providing evidence of gender-dependent social meanings and stylistic accommodation.

3. **Differences from the West?** While there is not enough evidence to claim that the discovered meanings of UPTALK in HKE are not also present in Western contexts, the patterns related to gender accommodation suggests that the interpretations of "femininity" in Hong Kong and Western contexts are different, leading to divergences in sociolinguistic uptalk patterning between contexts.

4. **The role of awareness.** Awareness plays a substantial role in UPTALK's social meaning. This is evident in both production and perception data. While there are many social meanings of UPTALK, in the context of Hong Kong, gendered meanings (e.g., feminine) alongside proficiency-related (e.g., lack of English proficiency) and ethnicity-based meanings (e.g., foreign-ness) tend to surface especially when participants are explicitly aware of the uptalk variable. Speakers use uptalk explicitly in style work, as evident in both production and perception data.

5. **Production–perception link.** The production and perception of UPTALK do not invariably align. Not all social meanings of UPTALK are perceptible or significant to speakers – for instance, its associations with mixed-gender groups or positivity. Moreover, while speakers may attribute specific meanings to uptalk, such as meanings of youth or belonging to lower/middle social classes, these attributions are not consistently reflected in their actual usage, as demonstrated by the minimal social variation observed. This discrepancy highlights that uptalk usage does not consistently adhere to societal expectations, underscoring the intricate processes through which language functions as a medium for identity construction.

Drawing on these pivotal insights, our study seeks to enrich sociolinguistic theory by demonstrating how social meanings and the indexical fields associated with them can function at multiple levels. Our analysis already reveals the complexity of UPTALK as a variable. However, by deconstructing uptalk into finer subvariables, such as rising intonation or tone variability, and examining the social meanings attributed to these more granular elements, we have uncovered that the fields of meaning for these subvariables can diverge significantly from those associated with the broader macrovariable of UPTALK.

The insights gleaned from this Element enhance our comprehension of sociolinguistics by emphasizing the necessity of integrating both production and perception data to comprehensively map the indexical fields of sociolinguistic variables. Existing scholarship on gender and language variation in Hong Kong (K.-L. J. Wong 2006; Chen & Kang 2015), and throughout the Asia-Pacific region (Dickson & Durantin 2019; Leimgruber et al. 2021) often adheres to an "either-or" methodology in variation analysis. Many studies prioritize corpus data alone, seeking to decode meanings through past research or self-interpretation. Conversely, other studies focus solely on evaluation data, without assessing whether these interpreted meanings are actively employed in stylistic practices. While research concentrating exclusively on production or evaluation provides valuable insights and lays groundwork for future investigations, a more comprehensive understanding necessitates an integrative approach. By embracing an "and" methodology, as demonstrated in this Element, we overcome the interpretative constraints inherent in the "either-or" approach, thereby yielding both analytical and theoretical advancements. Analyzing both production and evaluation facilitates a deeper, more reliable exploration of the social meanings associated with a variable, advancing our theoretical framework of sociolinguistic variation and social meaning.

Moreover, the findings of this Element are instrumental for advancing sociolinguistic theory by illustrating that the connections between linguistic variables and social meanings are frequently complex, resonating with current postmodernist trends in sociolinguistic research. These findings caution against the simplistic interpretation of sociolinguistic variables, such as presuming that they invariably correspond to ideological binaries (e.g., male vs. female), which might embody highly intricate meanings. While macrocategories are crucial for analyzing variation, it is essential to "complexify" our understanding of phenomena like uptalk to accurately reflect the inherent complexity of sociolinguistic variation and language itself (Gonzales 2024, 2025). This necessitates enhancing both our methodological approaches and our analyses, as demonstrated in this study. The Element underscores the importance of transcending macrocategories to also consider microvariations (e.g., individual differences, conversational dynamics) and the potential for interactions, which may be more important factors of variation than the ones we frequently encounter in sociolinguistic literature (e.g., gender and uptalk).

In summary, this study enriches our understanding of sociolinguistic variation by challenging conventional interpretations and advancing a nuanced approach to analyzing language variables like UPTALK in HKE. By embracing a holistic methodological framework that integrates both production and perception/evaluation analyses, our findings underscore the complex interplay of individual, social, and contextual factors in shaping linguistic practices. This approach not only sheds light on the subtle dynamics of gender and sociolinguistic variation but also prompts a reevaluation of how sociolinguistic meanings are constructed and perceived within a community. Through this comprehensive investigation, we advocate for a refined analytical lens in sociolinguistic research, emphasizing the importance of methodological rigor and theoretical flexibility in exploring the relationship between language and social meaning.

References

Agha, Asif. 2003. The social life of cultural value. *Language & Communication* 23(3–4): 231–73, https://doi.org/10.1016/S0271-5309(03)00012.

Bell, Allan. 1984. Language style as audience design. *Language in Society* 13(2): 145–204.

Blei, David M., Ng, Andrew Y., & Jordan, Michael I. 2003. Latent Dirichlet allocation. *Journal of Machine Learning Research* 3: 993–1022.

Britain, David. 1992. Linguistic change in intonation: The use of high rising terminals in New Zealand English. *Language Variation and Change* 4(1): 77–104, https://doi.org/10.1017/S0954394500000661.

Brown, Penelope & Levinson, Stephen C. 1987. *Politeness: Some Universals in Language Usage*. Cambridge: Cambridge University Press.

Bucholtz, Mary. 1999. "Why be normal?": Language and identity practices in a community of nerd girls. *Language in Society* 28(02): 203–23, https://doi.org/10.1017/S0047404599002043.

Bucholtz, Mary & Hall, Kira. 2005. Identity and interaction: A sociocultural linguistic approach. *Discourse Studies* 7(4–5): 585–614, https://doi.org/10.1177/1461445605054407.

Butler, Judith. 1988. Performative Acts and Gender Constitution: An Essay in Phenomenology and Feminist Theory. *Theatre Journal* 40(4): 519–31, https://doi.org/10.2307/3207893.

Calder, Jeremy. 2019. The fierceness of fronted /s/: Linguistic rhematization through visual transformation. *Language in Society* 48(1): 31–64, https://doi.org/10.1017/S004740451800115X.

Cameron, Deborah. 2003. Gender issues in language change. *Annual Review of Applied Linguistics* 23: 187–201, https://doi.org/10.1017/S0267190503000266.

Campbell-Kibler, Kathryn. 2010. The effect of speaker information on attitudes toward (ING). *Journal of Language and Social Psychology* 29(2): 214–23, https://doi.org/10.1177/0261927X09359527.

Cao, Juan, Xia, Tian, Li, Jintao, Zhang, Yongdong, & Tang, Sheng. 2009. A density-based method for adaptive LDA model selection. *Neurocomputing* 72(7–9): 1775–81, https://doi.org/10.1016/j.neucom.2008.06.011.

Carli, Linda L. 1990. Gender, language, and influence. *Journal of Personality and Social Psychology* 59(5): 941–51, https://doi.org/10.1037/0022-3514.59.5.941.

Chen, Katherine H. Y. & Kang, M. Agnes. 2015. Demeanor indexicals, interpretive discourses and the "Kong Girl" stereotype: Constructing gender ideologies in social media. *Journal of Language and Sexuality* 4(2): 193–222, https://doi.org/10.1075/jls.4.2.02che.

Cheng, Winnie & Warren, Martin. 2005. //CAN i help you //: The use of *rise* and *rise-fall* tones in the Hong Kong Corpus of Spoken English. *International Journal of Corpus Linguistics* 10(1): 85–107, https://doi.org/10.1075/ijcl.10.1.05che.

Cruwys, Tegan, Steffens, Niklas K., Haslam, S. Alexander, Haslam, Catherine, Jetten, Jolanda, & Dingle, Genevieve A. 2016. Social identity mapping: A procedure for visual representation and assessment of subjective multiple group memberships. *British Journal of Social Psychology* 55(4): 613–42, https://doi.org/10.1111/bjso.12155.

Dickson, Greg & Durantin, Gautier. 2019. Variation in the reflexive in Australian Kriol. *Asia-Pacific Language Variation* 5(2): 171–207.

Dodsworth, Robin M. 2005. Linguistic variation and sociological consciousness. PhD dissertation, Columbus, Ohio: The Ohio State University.

D'Onofrio, Annette. 2018. Controlled and automatic perceptions of a sociolinguistic marker. *Language Variation and Change* 30(2): 261–85, https://doi.org/10.1017/S095439451800008X.

D'Onofrio, Annette. 2020. Personae in sociolinguistic variation. *WIREs Cognitive Science* 11(6): e1543, https://doi.org/10.1002/wcs.1543.

Du Bois, John W. 2007. The stance triangle. In *Stancetaking in Discourse: Subjectivity, Evaluation, Interaction.* Pragmatics & Beyond New Series 164, Robert Englebretson (ed.), 139–82. Amsterdam: John Benjamins.

Eckert, Penelope. 1989. The whole woman: Sex and gender differences in variation. *Language Variation and Change* 1: 245–67.

Eckert, Penelope. 2008. Variation and the indexical field. *Journal of Sociolinguistics* 12(4): 453–76.

Eckert, Penelope. 2016. Variation, meaning, and change. In *Sociolinguistics: Theoretical Debates*, Nikolas Coupland (ed.), 68–85, Cambridge: Cambridge University Press.

Gadanidis, Timothy, Kiss, Angelika, Konnelly, Lex, Pabst, Katharina, Schlegl, Lisa, Umbal, Pocholo, & Tagliamonte, Sali A. 2023. Integrating qualitative and quantitative analyses of stance: A case study of English *that/*zero variation. *Language in Society 52(1):* 27-50, https://doi.org/10.1017/S0047404521000671.

Giles, Howard. 2016. *Communication Accommodation Theory: Negotiating Personal Relationships and Social Identities across Contexts*. Cambridge: Cambridge University Press, https://doi.org/10.1017/CBO9781316226537.

Glaser, Barney G. & Strauss, Anselm L. 2017. *The Discovery of Grounded Theory: Strategies for Qualitative Research.* 1st ed. Routledge, https://doi.org/10.4324/9780203793206.

Gonzales, Wilkinson Daniel Wong. 2024. The holistic advantage: Unified quantitative modeling for less-biased, in-depth insights into (socio)linguistic variation. *Languages* 9(5): 182, https://doi.org/10.3390/languages9050182.

Gonzales, Wilkinson Daniel Wong. 2025. *Our People's Language: Variation and Change in the Lánnang-Uè of the Manila Lannangs.* Amsterdam: John Benjamins.

Gratton, Chantal. 2016. Resisting the gender binary: The use of (ING) in the construction of non-binary transgender identities. *University of Pennsylvania Working Papers in Linguistics* 22(2): 51–60.

Guy, Gregory, Horvath, Barbara, Vonwiller, Julia, Daisley, Elaine, & Rogers, Inge. 1986. An intonational change in progress in Australian English. *Language in Society* 15(1): 23–51.

Haas, Ingrid J., Jones, Christopher R., & Fazio, Russell H. 2019. Social identity and the use of ideological categorization in political evaluation. *Journal of Social and Political Psychology* 7(1): 335–53, https://doi.org/10.5964/jspp.v7i1.790.

Hall-Lew, Lauren, Cardoso, Amanda, & Davies, Emma. 2021. Social meaning and sound change. In *Social Meaning and Linguistic Variation: Theorizing the Third Wave*, Lauren Hall-Lew, Emma Moore, & Robert J. Podesva (eds.), 27–53. Cambridge: Cambridge University Press, https://doi.org/10.1017/9781108578684.002.

Hall-Lew, Lauren, Moore, Emma, & Podesva, Robert J. (eds.). 2021. *Social Meaning and Linguistic Variation: Theorizing the Third Wave.* Cambridge University Press.

Hansen Edwards, Jette G. 2016. The politics of language and identity: Attitudes towards Hong Kong English pre and post the Umbrella Movement. *Asian Englishes* 18(2): 157–64, https://doi.org/10.1080/13488678.2016.1139937.

Hoffman, Michol F. & Walker, James A. 2010. Ethnolects and the city: Ethnic orientation and linguistic variation in Toronto English. *Language Variation and Change* 22(1): 37–67.

Innes, Bronwen. 2007. "Everything happened so quickly?" HRT intonation in New Zealand courtrooms. *Research on Language & Social Interaction* 40(2–3): 227–54, https://doi.org/10.1080/08351810701354672.

Johnstone, Barbara. 2017. Characterological figures and expressive style in the enregisterment of linguistic variety. In *Language and a Sense of Place*, Chris Montgomery & Emma Moore (eds.), 283–300. Cambridge: Cambridge University Press.

Kam, Lucetta Yip Lo. 2003. Negotiating gender masculine women in Hong Kong. Master's Thesis, Hong Kong, SAR, People's Republic of China: Chinese University of Hong Kong.

Kang, M. Agnes & Chen, Katherine Hoi Ying. 2017. Gender stereotype as a vehicle for social change? The case of the Kong Girl. *Gender and Language* 11(4): 460–81, https://doi.org/10.1558/genl.31607.

Kiesling, Scott F. 2005. Variation, stance and style: Word-final -*er*, high rising tone, and ethnicity in Australian English. *English World-Wide: A Journal of Varieties of English* 26(1): 1–42, https://doi.org/10.1075/eww.26.1.02kie.

Kiesling, Scott F. 2018. Masculine stances and the linguistics of affect: On masculine ease. *NORMA* 13(3–4): 191–212, https://doi.org/10.1080/18902138.2018.1431756.

Kiesling, Scott F. 2022. Stance and stancetaking. *Annual Review of Linguistics* 8(1): 409–26, https://doi.org/10.1146/annurev-linguistics-031120-121256.

Kish Bar-On, Kati & Lamm, Ehud. 2023. The interplay of social identity and norm psychology in the evolution of human groups. *Philosophical Transactions of the Royal Society B: Biological Sciences* 378(1872): 20210412, https://doi.org/10.1098/rstb.2021.0412.

Kursa, Miron B. & Rudnicki, Witold R. 2010. Feature selection with the Boruta package. *Journal of Statistical Software* 36(11): 1–13.

Labov, William. 1972a. *Sociolinguistic Patterns*. Philadelphia: University of Pennsylvania Press.

Labov, William. 1972b. The social motivation of a sound change. In *Sociolinguistic Patterns*, 251–65. New York: Academic.

Labov, William. 1984. The intersection of sex and social factors in the course of language change. Paper presentation presented at the NWAVE, Philadelphia.

Lakoff, Robin. 1973. Language and woman's place. *Language in Society* 2(1): 45–80.

Lam, Kwok Wai. 2020. *Intonational Variation in Hong Kong English*. Hong Kong, SAR, People's Republic of China: The Chinese University of Hong Kong.

Leaper, Campbell & Ayres, Melanie M. 2007. A meta-analytic review of gender variations in adults' language use: Talkativeness, affiliative speech, and assertive speech. *Personality and Social Psychology Review* 11(4): 328–63, https://doi.org/10.1177/1088868307302221.

Leimgruber, Jakob, Lim, Jun Jie, Gonzales, Wilkinson Daniel Wong, & Hiramoto, Mie. 2021. Ethnic and gender variation in the use of Colloquial Singapore English discourse particles. *English Language and Linguistics* 25(3): 601–20, https://doi.org/10.1017/S1360674320000453.

Levon, Erez. 2016. Gender, interaction and intonational variation: The discourse functions of high rising terminals in London. *Journal of Sociolinguistics* 20(2): 133–63, https://doi.org/10.1111/josl.12182.

Levon, Erez. 2020. Same difference: The phonetic shape of high rising terminals in London. *English Language and Linguistics* 24(1): 49–73, https://doi.org/10.1017/S1360674318000205.

Liong, Chan-ching Mario. 2010. Between responsibilities and privileges: The gender construction of fatherhood in Hong Kong. PhD dissertation, Hong Kong, SAR, People's Republic of China: Chinese University of Hong Kong.

Makowski, Dominique, Ben-Shachar, Mattan S., Chen, S. H. Annabel, & Lüdecke, Daniel. 2019. Indices of effect existence and significance in the Bayesian framework. *Frontiers in Psychology* 10: 2767, https://doi.org/10.3389/fpsyg.2019.02767.

Mallinson, Christine, Childs, Becky & Van Herk, Gerard. 2017. *Data Collection in Sociolinguistics*. New York: Routledge.

McKinley, Jim & Rose, Heath (eds.). 2020. *The Routledge Handbook of Research Methods in Applied Linguistics*. 1st ed. New York: Taylor and Francis, https://doi.org/10.4324/9780367824471.

Meyerhoff, Miriam. 2018. *Introducing Sociolinguistics*. 3rd ed. New York: Taylor and Francis.

Podesva, Robert J. 2007. Phonation type as a stylistic variable: The use of falsetto in constructing a persona. *Journal of Sociolinguistics* 11(4): 478–504, https://doi.org/10.1111/j.1467-9841.2007.00334.x.

Pratt, Teresa. 2021. Affect in sociolinguistic style. *Language in Society*, 1–26, https://doi.org/10.1017/S0047404521000774.

Prichard, Hilary & Tamminga, Meredith. 2012. The impact of higher education on Philadelphia vowels. *U. Penn Working Papers in Linguistics* 18(2): 87–95.

Rinker, Tyler. 2022. sentimentR. R, https://github.com/trinker/sentimentr.

Sauntson, Helen. 2019. *Researching Language, Gender and Sexuality: A Student Guide*. London: Routledge.

Schnurr, Stephanie & Mak, Bernie. 2011. Leadership in Hong Kong: Is gender really not an issue? *Gender and Language* 5(2): 337–64.

Shen, Yang. 2016. Filial daughters? Agency and subjectivity of rural migrant women in Shanghai. *The China Quarterly* 226: 519–37, https://doi.org/10.1017/S0305741016000357.

Slobe, Tyanna. 2018. Style, stance, and social meaning in mock white girl. *Language in Society* 47(4): 541–67, https://doi.org/10.1017/S004740451800060X.

Tyler, Joseph C. 2015. Expanding and mapping the indexical field: Rising pitch, the uptalk stereotype, and perceptual variation. *Journal of English Linguistics* 43(4): 284–310, https://doi.org/10.1177/0075424215607061.

Vehtari, Aki, Gelman, Andrew, Simpson, Daniel, Carpenter, Bob & Bürkner, Paul-Christian. 2021. Rank-normalization, folding, and localization: An improved $\hat{R}$ for assessing convergence of MCMC (with discussion). *Bayesian Analysis* 16(2): 667–718, https://doi.org/10.1214/20-BA1221.

Warren, Paul. 2015. *Uptalk: The Phenomenon of Rising Intonation*. 1st ed. Cambridge: Cambridge University Press, https://doi.org/10.1017/CBO9781316403570.

Wong, Kwok-Lan Jamie. 2004. Gender and codemixing in Hong Kong. Undergraduate, Australia: University of Sydney, http://hdl.handle.net/2123/1726.

Wong, Kwok-Lan Jamie. 2006. Gender and codemixing in Hong Kong. Master's thesis, Department of Linguistics, http://hdl.handle.net/2123/1726.

Wong, Yin Ping. 2018. Saying no: An investigation of Hong Kong tertiary learners' pragmatic competency on refusal. Bachelor's thesis, Hong Kong, SAR, People's Republic of China: The Education University of Hong Kong.

Cambridge Elements

Language, Gender and Sexuality

Helen Sauntson
York St John University

Helen Sauntson is Professor of English Language and Linguistics at York St John University, UK. Her research areas are language in education and language, gender and sexuality. She is co-editor of *The Palgrave Studies in Language, Gender and Sexuality* book series, and she sits on the editorial boards of the journals *Gender and Language* and the *Journal of Language and Sexuality*. Within her institution, Helen is Director of the Centre for Language and Social Justice Research.

Editorial Board
Lilian Lem Atanga, *The University of Bamenda*
Eva Nossem, *Saarland University*
Joshua M. Paiz, *The George Washington University*
M. Agnes Kang, *University of Hong Kong*

About the Series
Cambridge Elements in Language, Gender and Sexuality highlights the role of language in understanding issues, identities and relationships in relation to multiple genders and sexualities. The series provides a comprehensive home for key topics in the field which readers can consult for up-to-date coverage and the latest developments.

Cambridge Elements ≡

Language, Gender and Sexuality

Elements in the Series

The Language of Gender-Based Separatism
Veronika Koller, Alexandra Krendel and Jessica Aiston

Queering Sexual Health Translation Pedagogy
Piero Toto

Legal Categorization of 'Transgender': An Analysis of Statutory Interpretation of 'Sex', 'Man', and 'Woman' in Transgender Jurisprudence
Kimberly Tao

LGBTQ+ and Feminist Digital Activism: A Linguistic Perspective
Angela Zottola

Feminism, Corpus-assisted Research and Language Inclusivity
Federica Formato

Queering Language Revitalisation: Navigating Identity and Inclusion among Queer Speakers of Minority Languages
John Walsh, Michael Hornsby, Eva J. Daussà, Renée Pera-Ros, Samuel Parker, Jonathan Morris and Holly R. Cashman

Pride in Asia: Negotiating Ideologies, Localness, and Alternative Futures
Benedict J. L. Rowlett, Pavadee Saisuwan, Christian Go,
Li-Chi Chen and Mie Hiramoto

Language, Gender and Pregnancy Loss
Beth Malory

Discourse and Queer Sinophone Male Identities: A Western Immigrant Perspective
Phil Freestone

Linguistic Representations of Women in Old English Prose: A Corpus-Based Phraseological Study
Anna Cichosz and Tomasz Dobrogoszcz

Language, Gender and Biopolitics: Meaning-Making and Intersex Variations in Healthcare
Brian W. King

Gender and Uptalk in Hong Kong English
Wilkinson Daniel Wong Gonzales, Chan Pui Yu Ivy, Zhang Xiaohan Harry, Ng Chui Yin Judy and Chung Yan Ching Karina

A full series listing is available at: www.cambridge.org/ELGS

For EU product safety concerns, contact us at Calle de José Abascal, 56–1º,
28003 Madrid, Spain or eugpsr@cambridge.org.